About This Book

Why is this topic important?

A well-trained workforce is essential for success in a competitive global economy. Designing and developing training programs requires a wide range of skills and knowledge, yet the responsibility for providing training often falls on people with little or no experience in the field. People who are new to training and those with limited experience need easily accessible information and practical tools that help them understand the instructional design process so that they can get up to speed quickly.

What can you achieve with this book?

In today's rapidly changing organizations, people need to be able to do more with fewer resources. Those who are new to training do not have the luxury of time in which to learn about the various instructional design methods and approaches to providing training. This book is an easy-to-use resource that provides practical information, best practices, proven strategies, tips, and tools for designing and developing training programs that achieve results.

How is this book organized?

The book begins with an overview of the most commonly used instructional design process. The subsequent chapters provide detailed how-to information about how to carry out each step in the process, from analyzing the need for training and writing training objectives through developing program materials and designing a program evaluation. Each chapter includes questions and application activities to enhance learning. At the back of the book is a list of resources for learning more.

About Pfeiffer

Pfeiffer serves the professional development and hands-on resource needs of training and human resource practitioners and gives them products to do their jobs better. We deliver proven ideas and solutions from experts in HR development and HR management, and we offer effective and customizable tools to improve workplace performance. From novice to seasoned professional, Pfeiffer is the source you can trust to make yourself and your organization more successful.

Essential Knowledge Pfeiffer produces insightful, practical, and comprehensive materials on topics that matter the most to training and HR professionals. Our Essential Knowledge resources translate the expertise of seasoned professionals into practical, how-to guidance on critical workplace issues and problems. These resources are supported by case studies, worksheets, and job aids and are frequently supplemented with CD-ROMs, websites, and other means of making the content easier to read, understand, and use.

Essential Tools Pfeiffer's Essential Tools resources save time and expense by offering proven, ready-to-use materials—including exercises, activities, games, instruments, and assessments—for use during a training or team-learning event. These resources are frequently offered in looseleaf or CD-ROM format to facilitate copying and customization of the material.

Pfeiffer also recognizes the remarkable power of new technologies in expanding the reach and effectiveness of training. While e-hype has often created whizbang solutions in search of a problem, we are dedicated to bringing convenience and enhancements to proven training solutions. All our e-tools comply with rigorous functionality standards. The most appropriate technology wrapped around essential content yields the perfect solution for today's on-the-go trainers and human resource professionals.

Essential resources for training and HR professionals

Designing and Developing Training Programs

Pfeiffer Essential Guides to Training Basics

Janis Fisher Chan

Published by Pfeiffer
An Imprint of Wiley
989 Market Street, San Francisco, CA 94103-1741
www.pfeiffer.com

For additional copies/bulk purchases of this book in the U.S. please contact 800-274-4434.
Pfeiffer books and products are available through most bookstores. To contact Pfeiffer directly call our Customer Care Department within the U.S. at 800-274-4434, outside the U.S. at 317-572-3985, fax 317-572-4002, or visit www.pfeiffer.com.

Pfeiffer also publishes its books in a variety of electronic formats. Some content that appears in print may not be available in electronic books.

Library of Congress Cataloging-in-Publication Data

Chan, Janis Fisher.
Designing and developing training programs / Janis Fisher Chan.
p. cm.—(Pfeiffer essential guides to training basics)
Includes bibliographical references and index.
ISBN 978-0-470-40469-0 (pbk.)
1. Employees—Training of. 2. Employee training personnel. 3. Training. I. Title.
HF5549.5.T7C5338 2010
658.3'124—dc22

2009031950

Acquiring Editor: Matthew Davis
Production Editor: Dawn Kilgore
Editorial Assistant: Lindsay Morton

Director of Development: Kathleen Dolan Davies
Editor: Rebecca Taff
Manufacturing Supervisor: Becky Morgan

Printed in the United States of America

Printing 10 9 8 7 6 5 4 3 2

Contents

Introduction

My first job in the training field was for a company that had just received a large contract to design and develop learning programs for the U.S. Army. I knew nothing about the Army, and nothing about training. Neither did any of my colleagues. We had all been hired because we knew how to write and were interested in the learning process. And that's the first thing we did: we learned. No one taught us about adult learning principles or educational theory. Instead, we learned the instructional design process by taking a self-paced learning program in which we developed a self-paced learning program of our own (mine was to teach my husband how to balance a checking account). Once we "graduated," we immediately took our learning into the "real" world, where we applied it by designing, developing, testing, and evaluating training programs to meet our clients' specific needs and objectives.

The fundamentals of the instructional design process I learned at that job have stayed with me, providing the foundation for my career as a training professional. But I learned more than a process. I learned a basic truth about training: that people learn best not by listening to someone tell them what to do, but by doing things themselves. That basic truth is a key theme for this book.

About the Pfeiffer Essential Guides to Training Basics

The three books in this series, *Training Fundamentals, Designing and Developing Training Programs*, and *Delivering Training Workshops*, provide practical ideas, information, tips, and techniques for people who are new to the training field as well as trainers who have been in the field for a while and would like to learn more.

Training Fundamentals

This book is a no-nonsense, practical overview of training. Here's what you'll learn:

- What training is and the role it plays in helping organizations achieve their goals

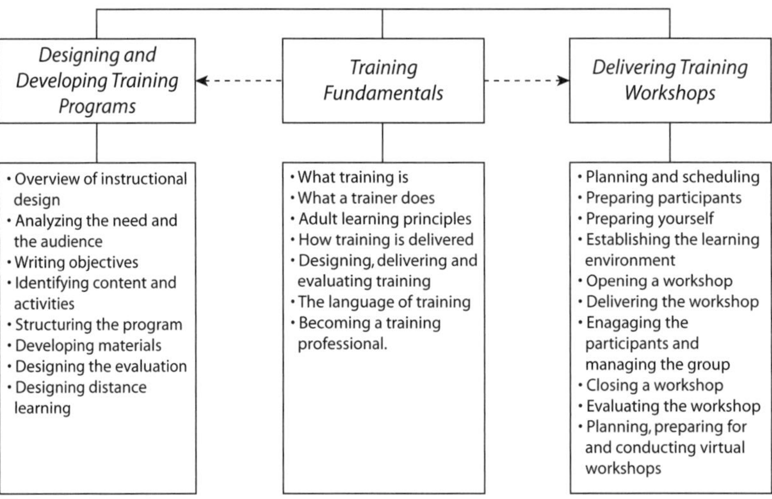

- What a trainer does and the characteristics and skills a trainer needs to be successful
- The ways in which training is delivered
- The adult learning principles that guide successful training programs
- What's involved in designing training to meet specific needs, delivering a training workshop, and evaluating training success
- The terminology and acronyms commonly used in the training field
- How you can develop yourself as a training professional.

Designing and Developing Training Programs

Building on the basics provided in *Training Fundamentals*, this book guides you through the instructional design process, providing practical ideas, information, tools, and strategies you can use immediately. You'll learn how to:

- Make sure that training is needed, relevant, and cost-effective
- Analyze the needs and characteristics of the audience

- Write the behavioral learning objectives that provide the foundation for a training program
- Decide what content to include
- Select activities that engage people and help them learn
- Organize content and activities into a workable structure
- Develop trainer's guides, participant workbooks, slide presentations, and other learning materials
- Design a program evaluation
- Design virtual and remote training programs.

Delivering Training Workshops

Also building on the basics of delivery presented in *Training Fundamentals*, this book provides strategies, best practices, tips, and guidelines you can use immediately to prepare for, deliver, and follow up on a workshop. You'll learn how to:

- Plan and schedule a workshop
- Prepare participants so they know what to expect and arrive ready to learn
- Increase your confidence by preparing yourself to conduct training
- Establish an environment that is conducive to learning
- Get started in a way that immediately engages participants
- Present information clearly, keep people involved, and respond to questions
- Manage the group and keep the workshop on track
- Close a workshop in a way that helps participants use what they learn
- Evaluate the success of a workshop
- Plan, prepare for, and conduct virtual workshops

How to Use This Book

This book expands on and adds to the concepts and ideas presented in *Training Fundamentals*, so if you have read that book, you will find some of the information familiar. The focus in that book, however, was to provide an overview of the training design and development process, while this book provides greater detail and practical techniques for putting the process to use.

Like the other two books in the series, this book is designed as a learning tool. You'll find questions and suggested activities that will help you think about what you are learning, make connections between new learning and what you already know, and apply what you learn. The answers to the questions are either apparent in the text or appear at the end of the chapter. I encourage you to answer the questions and do the activities, but feel free to skip any that don't seem relevant. In other words, this is your book; use it the way that works best for you.

Check What You Know

When you see this icon, you'll find questions that help you see what you already know about the topic or subtopic.

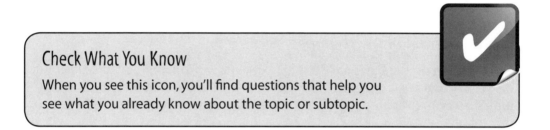

THINK ABOUT IT

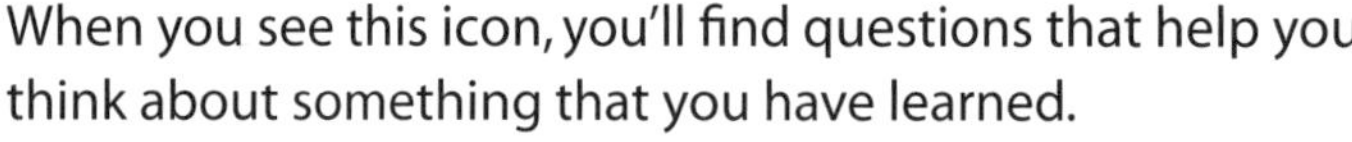

When you see this icon, you'll find questions that help you think about something that you have learned.

Quick Quiz

From time to time, you'll find a quiz that will help you check your understanding of the material.

Apply What You Learn

When you see this icon, you'll find questions or an activity to help you apply the learning to a real situation.

Before You Begin

One theme that you'll find throughout the *Training Basics* series is the importance of helping people apply what they learn in training to real-world situations. That's the purpose of the activities that you will find at the ends of most of the chapters—to help you apply the learning to a training project of your own.

Choose a project that you can think about as you read this book and describe it below. The project should be a training program that you need to design and develop. If you have no real, current project to work on, think of a training program that you could provide for people at your company or for people at another organization, such as a nonprofit or community group.

Briefly describe your training program:

____

____

Who is the audience for this program?

____

____

Why is this program needed? What is it intended to accomplish?

____

____

Your Objectives

Another important theme that you will find in each book of the series is that it's easier to get somewhere when you know where you are going. Think about what you would like to accomplish by reading this book and briefly describe your objectives below:

1

The Training Plan

Check What You Know

The CEO of Account Services, which provides payroll, bookkeeping, and accounting services to small and medium-sized businesses in several states, is unhappy with the employees' use of e-mail. "They don't know how to write," she told the human resources manager. "Some of the stuff they're sending out is embarrassing. And look at this. One of our best clients got this e-mail from someone in billing last week."

The HR manager read the e-mail that the CEO handed him, shocked to find a very offensive remark in the second line. "That kind of thing could land us in court," he said.

The CEO agreed. "That's one of my concerns," she said. "But I'm also worried about our relationships with our clients. Positive relationships are crucial to our business, and so many of them know us only through e-mail exchanges. And it's not only clients. Some of the internal e-mail I've seen is a mess—I've been copied on messages that made no sense at all. We can't afford having people waste time reading and writing useless messages."

"What would you like me to do?" the HR manager asked.

"I know you and your staff are busy with the new hire program. But I see fixing this problem as a top priority. Could you carve out some time to put

(*Continued*)

together some training? A workshop, or something, to make sure that people are using e-mail to get our business done, not to send out messages like this one."

That afternoon, the human resources manager looked through some of the e-mail messages that employees in various parts of the company had written and talked with a few managers about their employees' use of e-mail. The next morning, he called two new associates, Boris and Marietta, into his office and explained the situation.

"The CEO isn't happy with the way people are using e-mail, and she wants us to put together a workshop. All the other associates are swamped with the new hire program. Is this something you two would like to take on?"

Boris and Marietta looked at each other. "Sure," they said, almost in unison.

"Good." The HR manager handed them the samples he'd printed out the day before, along with the notes from his conversations with the managers. "These will help you get started." He opened his calendar. "Do you think you can get me some ideas within three weeks?"

As they walked down the hall toward their cubicles, Boris said, "Have you ever put together a training program before?"

"Nope," Marietta replied. "But I took lots of workshops at my last job. And I taught high school algebra for a year, with the Teach For America program. How hard could it be?"

How hard, indeed? Boris and Marietta are about to find out.

What if you were advising Boris and Marietta? What do you think their first step needs to be?

____

____

____

____

Many of the things we do in life begin with an idea: Let's go to Hawaii. Let's open a business. Let's add a room to our house. In the scenario that began this chapter, the Account Services CEO had an idea—let's have some e-mail training.

Implicit in the idea is that something needs to change or be improved, along with a typically vague understanding of the desired outcome. Let's go to Hawaii because we've been working too hard and a vacation on the beach will help us relax. Let's open a business because we need some extra income. Let's add a room to our house because our children need rooms of their own. Let's have an e-mail workshop because people are wasting time and sending e-mail that embarrasses the company.

But having an idea is one thing—turning it into reality is another. The path to the destination can be filled with obstacles and surprises. To get there without wasting valuable time and other resources, you need a plan.

Here's what's in this chapter:

- Why you need a plan
- ADDIE—a model for planning instructional programs
- What to consider when using the ADDIE process

Instruction is only one of several possible solutions to problems of human performance, and not even the one most often called for. . . . It is possible to construct a course that nobody needs, either because instruction is unrelated to solving the problem that gave rise to it, or because it "teaches" things the students already know.

Robert F. Mager,
Preparing Instructional Objectives

1. Why You Need a Plan

Check What You Know

The HR manager asked Boris and Marietta to put together a plan to meet the CEO's request for an e-mail workshop. Why do they need a plan? What will a plan help them do?

____

____

____

____

I've known a number of people who have started successful businesses. One friend opened a children's clothing store. Another realized a life-long dream when she started a small restaurant. Others have started gardening businesses, web-design and publishing companies, bookkeeping firms, and day care programs. Those entrepreneurs didn't just leap from idea to success—they knew that a successful business doesn't just happen. Instead, they began with a plan that described their goals in detail and laid out specific steps for achieving them. They evaluated the feasibility of their ideas in the marketplace; figured out what money, time, expertise, and other resources they would need, how to obtain them, and how to make the best use of them; calculated the potential return on their investment; identified possible obstacles; and made action plans and checklists for all the tasks that needed to be done. Along the way, they made significant changes to their original ideas as they discovered better ways to accomplish their goals.

To succeed in today's highly competitive, rapidly changing environment, organizations have an increasing need for training that helps their employees work more productively and increases their ability to retain top performers. But they can't afford to waste scarce resources on training that is thrown together on a whim or costly programs that fail to accomplish meaningful goals. Instructional designers who neglect the planning process risk embarking on a project that wastes valuable resources without achieving a worthwhile outcome, disappointing and frustrating everyone involved, and leaving the organization worse off than it was before.

As Rosemary Caffarella says in her book, *Planning Programs for Adult Learners*, the assumption underlying education and training programs is that something needs to change. Careful planning is the way that instructional designers identify what change is needed (and whether it is needed), what the outcome of change will be, how important it is to achieve that outcome, whether training is the best way to achieve it, and what exactly needs to be done to move from idea to reality. Without planning, a training project can be like climbing aboard an engine that has no shutoff switch but is going nowhere. The only way to get off is to jump.

2. Planning Instructional Programs

The instructional systems design (ISD) process and training are means, not ends. Focusing on results, rather than focusing on providing training, causes decisions to be made in very different ways. The training development organization needs to be project-driven vs. being process- and control-driven.

Darryl L. Sink, "ISD—Faster/Better/Easier," in T.L. Gargiulo, A.M. Pangarkar, and T. Kirkwood (Eds.),
The Trainer's Portable Mentor

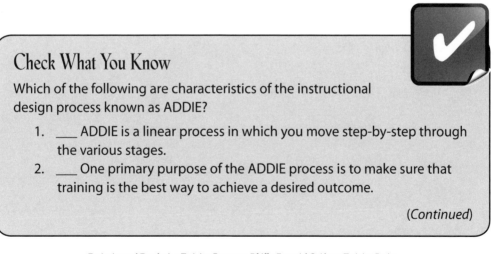

Check What You Know

Which of the following are characteristics of the instructional design process known as ADDIE?

1. ___ ADDIE is a linear process in which you move step-by-step through the various stages.
2. ___ One primary purpose of the ADDIE process is to make sure that training is the best way to achieve a desired outcome.

(Continued)

3. ___ An important reason for using ADDIE is that it has both structure and flexibility.
4. ___ The most time-consuming part of the ADDIE instructional design process is determining the best way to deliver training.
5. ___ The ADDIE process can be used to guide an organization's entire training effort or to plan training to meet a specific need.

Although there are different ways in which to approach the instructional design process, most instructional designers use some form of the model commonly known as ADDIE. Like so many others in the training field, I've found that ADDIE—which stands for Analysis, Design, Development, Implementation, and Evaluation—has both the structure and the flexibility to keep me on the right track and make sure that my training projects achieve my clients' goals. The model is shown below.

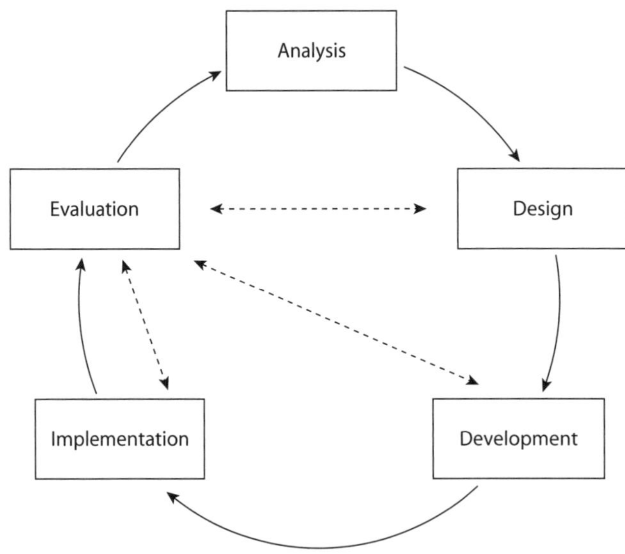

The ADDIE Model

ADDIE, which is sometimes referred to as "ISD," for "Instructional Systems Design," is based on an instructional systems approach to solving training problems that was established by the U.S. Department of Defense, which has a significant and ongoing need to train large numbers of people—and train them well. Because the letters of the acronym appear in order, it's easy to think that ADDIE is a rigid, linear process. Far from it: the process is designed to be dynamic and interactive, with evaluation and feedback at every step of the way. Depending on the situation, you might skip steps, do steps in a different order, and return to earlier steps in light of new information. As you use this planning process in different kinds of situations, you'll find that it is an extremely flexible method for approaching the essential tasks and decisions in the instructional design process.

ADDIE can be used to guide an organization's entire training effort, provide training for a team, or plan a training program to meet one specific need. In this book, you will learn the basics of the process by studying how it is used to design and develop a program to meet one training need.

Below is a brief description of each of the ADDIE stages. In the following chapters, you will learn about each stage in detail. (If you have read the first book in this series, *Training Fundamentals*, or are otherwise familiar with this process, you can read the following as a refresher or skip ahead to Chapter 2.)

Analysis

People who start their own businesses, like the friends I described earlier, begin the planning process by asking questions, such as:

- Why am I undertaking this project?
- What's the chance of succeeding?
- What does success look like?
- What do I need to do to achieve my goals?

The answers to those questions help them decide whether—and how—to move forward with their idea.

For a training program, one of the most important reasons for the analysis stage is to determine what change is needed, how important it is, and whether there is an easier, less costly way than training to achieve it. The instructional designer's key questions might include:

- What's the current situation? What is the desired outcome?
- What would happen if nothing were done?
- What's the best way of closing the gap between the current situation and the desired outcome?
- What are the needs, characteristics, and preferences of the people who are to be trained?
- Who has a stake in this training?
- What resources are available? What constraints must be considered?
- Who needs to be involved in the process of designing the program?

I mentioned earlier that you could skip steps in ADDIE. Let me revise that statement: You can't skip the analysis stage. In many cases, it doesn't have to take long or be very complicated—a few questions can provide enough information to decide whether and how to move forward. But even when the analysis stage requires a lot of time, it's worth it, because the information gathered in this stage provides a solid foundation for the entire project, shaping its scope and direction.

Design

Builders do not start constructing a house by picking up boards from a pile of lumber and hammering them together. They need detailed plans—blueprints and specifications—to guide them through the construction process so that the resulting structure meets all the design and structural requirements. For a training project, you will use the design document or outline that emerges from this stage of the ADDIE process as a guide for developing a program that achieves the intended outcomes and is instructionally sound. The "blueprint" for a training program describes what people will be able to do when training is completed; the training methodology; the content the program will cover; the activities that will be used to help people learn; and the ways in which the program will be evaluated.

Development

In this stage, you will develop, manage the development of, and/or purchase everything needed to run the training program—trainer materials, participant materials, software, videos, assessments, props—whatever the program requires. This is nearly always the most time-consuming part of the process. It can take hours or even days of work to develop a one-day workshop, and weeks or months to develop e-learning modules. To use time, money, expertise, and other resources as efficiently as possible, it's very important not to begin development without a detailed, well-thought-out program design.

The last part of this stage is testing, or validating, the program to make sure that everything works as planned and to identify changes that need to be made before the program is "rolled out." Whether to test the program informally or hold a formal pilot depends on its size, scope, and importance, as well as on the time and budget you have available.

Implementation

All the hard work done to design and develop the training program pays off when it's rolled out to the learners. There are lots of tasks in this stage—everything from scheduling training and arranging for equipment and facilities to notifying participants and preparing for training, not to mention delivering the program. Depending on your specific responsibilities, you might or might not have an active role to play in this stage.

Evaluation

Training isn't over when participants complete the program, and evaluation isn't a one-shot deal. Like analysis, this stage of ADDIE is the one that instructional designers most often skip, or do in a perfunctory way, yet it is one of the most important. Ongoing assessment and evaluation are crucial to making sure that training is relevant, effective, and provides a good return on investment. The information gathered during this stage helps organizations improve existing training programs and develop more effective training in the future.

3. What to Consider When Using ADDIE

ADDIE is a tool, not a procedure. It's a means to an end—the idea is not to follow the process "correctly," but to use it to achieve a specific outcome. As mentioned earlier, you won't necessarily do the steps in order, and in some situations you won't need to do all of them. You will often go back to earlier steps in light of new information—in fact, what you learn during the design or development stage might completely change your perception of the need and how to meet it. The process works best when you keep an open mind and remain willing to rethink your original ideas.

To make the best use of the ADDIE process, keep these suggestions in mind:

- *Pay enough attention to analysis.* As mentioned earlier, instructional designers tend to skip this stage, or not to complete it fully, especially when there are limited resources and a sense of urgency. They assume that because someone has asked for training, training is really needed. They act on information they are given without checking to make sure that it is accurate and complete. Yet when a training program fails to achieve the desired outcome or to prove worth the investment of time and resources, it's nearly always because no one bothered to do an analysis or because the analysis was incomplete.
- *Collect the right information.* You are probably familiar with the acronym "GIGO"—"garbage in, garbage out," referring to the fact that if you put a lot of nonsensical information into a computer, you're likely to get a lot of nonsensical information back. The process of designing and developing a successful training program requires gathering lots of information. But just doing a lot of research doesn't guarantee success. If the information on which you base the program design is inaccurate, incomplete, or outdated, the program is unlikely to achieve its goals. Gathering the right information means talking to the right people; asking the right questions; reading the right documents; observing people who are doing the job the right way, not the way they think it is supposed to be done; clarifying to make sure that you've understood what you are seeing, hearing, and reading; and discriminating between facts and assumptions, objective information and opinions.

THINK ABOUT IT

Have you ever put a lot of work into a project only to have a decision-maker tell you that it wasn't what he or she had in mind and ask you to make substantial changes? Why do you think that happened? What could you have done to reduce the chances that you would have to go back to the drawing board after you'd already done so much work?

____

____

____

____

____

____

- *Involve everyone who needs to be involved.* It's surprising how much work sometimes goes into the process of designing and developing a training program before the instructional designers have even bothered to discuss it with key stakeholders, especially those whose approval is needed before the program is rolled out. There are always lots of reasons for not bringing stakeholders into the process at an early stage: "They're too busy"; "There's nothing to show them yet"; "They don't want to see anything until it's all ready to go." But not involving key stakeholders early means that you can waste a lot of time going in the wrong direction and end up not meeting expectations.
- *As soon as you begin a training project, identify the key stakeholders whose assistance, support, and approval you will need for the project to succeed.* Those people always include anyone who has decision-making authority over

To Consider When Using ADDIE

- Pay enough attention to analysis, even if resources are limited and there is a sense of urgency.
- Get the right information—accurate, complete, and up-to-date.
- Involve everyone who needs to be involved—bring key stakeholders in early and keep them informed.
- If you come into a project that's already underway, confirm what's already been done—make sure the program design is sound.
- Keep an open mind and be willing to change direction when things change or you uncover new information.
- Be realistic—consider real-world issues and constraints.

Boris and Marietta's Progress

Boris and Marietta have been on a steep learning curve. They've talked with some experienced training professionals and read up on the instructional design process. Now they're ready to start on a plan to take to the HR manager. They meet over lunch in the company cafeteria to discuss what they need to do.

"It's clear to me where we have to begin," Marietta says. "We don't know enough about the situation. All we have is the CEO's request for a workshop, a stack of e-mail messages, and the HR director's notes."

"Right," Boris says. "We can't do anything until we have more information. So our first task is to find out how extensive this need is and whether a workshop is really the way to tackle it."

the program. They might also include the individual or the team who requested the training, your manager, the human resources or learning and development manager, important customers, and others. Make sure the stakeholders know that you will expect their review at important checkpoints during the process, and that you will move forward only after you have their approval.

- *If you come into a project that's already underway, review what's already been done*. In many cases, you will join a project after a certain amount of work has already been done. For example, the need might already have been analyzed and the program designed by the time you arrive on the scene. Your role might only be to develop the program. Before starting the tasks that fall into your area of responsibility, review what was done in earlier stages, such as the results of the analysis and the learning objectives. Make sure that the training need and desired outcome were clearly identified and the program design is sound before you begin work.
- *Keep an open mind and be willing to change direction*. When you design and develop a training program, you are continually collecting information, analyzing it, and comparing it to the information you already have. At any stage of the process, new information about the situation, the learners, or the topic can stop you in your tracks, forcing you to rethink your original perceptions and ideas. In fact, one of the advantages of the ADDIE process is that ongoing assessment and evaluation are built in at every step of the way. But it's essential to remain flexible, willing to jettison unworkable ideas no matter how much you might like them or how hard you've worked to come up with them, willing even to go back to the very beginning and start the process again.
- *Be realistic*. It's great to imagine wildly and think in terms of ideals. But in the real world, there are real issues and real constraints to consider when you are planning a training program. An e-learning program might be the best way to meet the need, but if there isn't enough time or money to develop one, you'll have to find another way. The desired outcome could be achieved most efficiently with a self-study workbook, but the manager who controls the budget insists that his team needs a workshop. The organization has a perfectly usable training program that could be adapted for the current need, but a key decision-maker wants a new one developed from scratch. As a training professional, you need to work with the situation that you have, not the one you want.

Quick Quiz

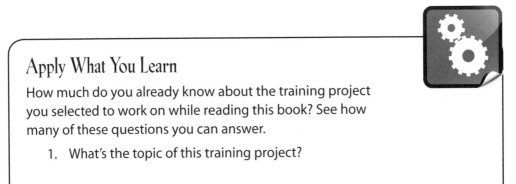

List the three to five key learning points from this chapter that will be most helpful to you.

____

____

____

____

____

What's Next?

It's during the analysis stage of ADDIE that you make sure that training is really needed and build a firm foundation for a training program. That's what you'll learn to do in the next chapter.

Apply What You Learn

How much do you already know about the training project you selected to work on while reading this book? See how many of these questions you can answer.

1. What's the topic of this training project?

____

2. Who are the learners?

3. What's the desired outcome?

4. Has the delivery method been selected? If so, what is it?

5. Who are the stakeholders?

6. What's the budget?

7. When does this program need to be ready?

8. What issues and constraints do you need to keep in mind?

9. What other factors might influence or affect this program?

Answers to Exercise

Check What You Know

Which of the following are characteristics of the instructional design process known as ADDIE?

1. ___ ADDIE is a linear process in which you move step-by-step through the various stages.
2. _X_ One primary purpose of the ADDIE process is to make sure that training is the best way to achieve a desired outcome.
3. _X_ An important reason for using ADDIE is that it has both structure and flexibility.
4. ___ The most time-consuming part of the ADDIE instructional design process is determining the best way to deliver training.
5. _X_ The ADDIE process can be used to guide an organization's entire training effort or to plan training to meet a specific need.

2

Analyzing the Situation

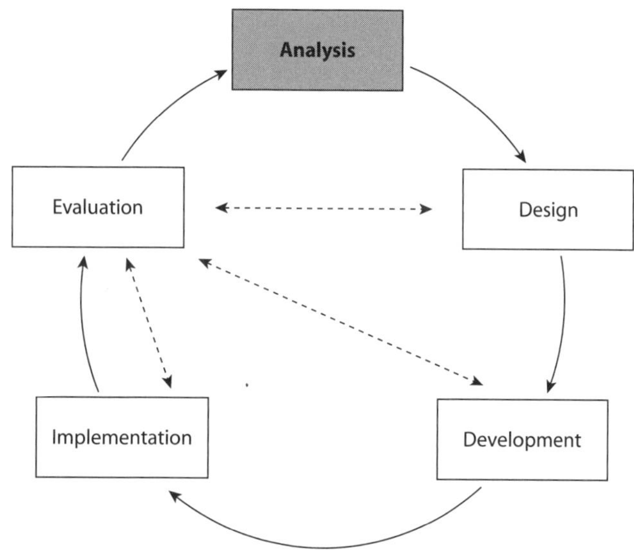

Analysis Stage of the ADDIE Model

Check What You Know

All the training professionals Boris and Marietta talked to and all the instructional design experts whose books they read said much the same thing: The first step is to collect enough information

(*Continued*)

to make sure that there is a real need for training. For Boris and Marietta, that means reading lots of e-mail messages and asking lots of questions about the ways in which people are using e-mail.

If you were advising Boris and Marietta, what are some of the questions you would suggest that they ask?

____

____

____

____

____

____

My husband and I have been thinking about putting a solar array on our roof to take advantage of our home's southern exposure and contribute to the greening of America. After consulting with a solar energy company, we called several roofing companies to find out whether we should replace our roof before installing solar panels. Two of the three companies said, "Yes, you should." But they hadn't seen our roof; they didn't even ask any questions about how long we've had it and what shape it was in—they just offered a quote for replacing it.

But the person we spoke to at the third company asked several questions about what we planned to do and then called someone at the solar energy company to ask more questions of the people there. Then she sent someone out to take a look.

The roofer examined the condition of the roof, looking for damage and signs of leakage. When he came down, he asked us to describe any problems that we'd had. When he finished his assessment, he told us that the roof was in reasonably good shape. We could install the solar panels on the existing roof (less expensive in the short run but likely to cost more when the roof does need to be replaced in five to seven years), or replace the portion of the roof on which the panels would be installed (reducing the risk that installing the panels would cause roof problems, which would necessitate moving the stanchions).

We haven't installed the solar panels yet, but we have made one important decision: when we do replace the roof, we'll go with the third company. Their thoughtful analysis of the situation will help us make an informed decision about the best way to achieve our objective—and avoid wasting money on a roof replacement that we don't really need.

That same kind of analysis is exactly what organizations need to do in order to save time and money on training. That's what you'll learn about in this chapter.

In this chapter:

- What's involved in assessing the need
- Gathering and analyzing the information
- Identifying the stakeholders
- Considering the learners' characteristics
- Identifying constraints and other factors that affect the design
- Determining who to involve in the design process
- Deciding whether to develop or purchase the program

1. What's a Needs Assessment?

. . . we must never lose our childlike fascination with creation. However . . . we are learning and performance professionals. Our mission is to produce results. We cannot afford the luxury of endlessly building artifacts that will sit on shelves.

Harold D. Stolovitch, "Front-End Analysis, Implementation Planning, and Evaluation," in T.M. Gargiulo, A.M. Pangarkar, and T. Kirkwood (Eds.), *The Trainer's Portable Mentor*

Needs assessment is often compared to the process of diagnosing an illness, and for good reason. When you come into the doctor's office complaining of a sore throat and fever, the doctor doesn't take your word for it that you need antibiotics. Before deciding what action to take, she analyzes the situation by asking questions, examining your throat, and running some tests. That doctor has just performed a needs assessment. Her objective is to go beyond the symptoms and determine what's really going on so she can prescribe the treatment that is most likely to help you get better.

Just as carefully diagnosing a medical problem is essential for determining the best way to treat it, carefully analyzing an apparent training need is essential for determining what action to take. In Chapter 1, you learned that implicit in the idea that training is needed is the assumption that something needs to be changed. The purpose of a training needs assessment is to gain enough understanding of the situation so that you can make informed decisions about whether change is really needed and whether training is the best way to achieve the desired outcome. The process is like putting together a puzzle or assembling clues until a clear picture emerges.

There are two general categories of needs assessments. The first, which I'll call "organizational" needs assessments, are large-scale analyses of changes in knowledge, skills, and attitudes that are needed for an organization to achieve its goals. The second, which I'll call "training" needs assessments, are more focused analyses that are intended to determine whether training is the best way to meet a need that has already been identified. Let's look a little more closely at the key differences.

Organizational Needs Assessment

Organizational needs assessments are conducted to determine what kinds of interventions, including training, are needed to help the organization achieve its strategic goals. The result is usually a series of actions, including training programs on a variety of topics, which are then prioritized according to urgency and importance.

This type of needs assessment, which can be conducted for an entire organization or for any department, team, or unit within it, requires gathering a great deal of information about the current situation, such as what people know, what they are able to do, how they behave, the ways in which they carry out specific tasks, and their attitudes. That information is then compared to what they need to know and be able to do for the organization to achieve its goals. The analysis helps the organization determine what learning and performance gaps exist, find both training and non-training solutions to problems, make sure that training efforts are aligned with the organization's strategic goals and vision, identify development opportunities, establish priorities, determine who should be involved in training efforts, and more.

Full-scale organizational needs assessments can take months, even years, to complete. Because they can be so complex, time-consuming, and costly, they are usually conducted by experienced training and organizational development professionals. Although a detailed discussion of the process is beyond the scope of this book, a good understanding of what organizational needs assessments are and the various methods for conducting them is useful to anyone involved in the training field. To learn more, see the Resources section at the back of this book.

Training Needs Assessment

The first question I ask regarding [designing effective instructional systems] is: Who says these are needs?

Bob Pike,
Creative Training Techniques

Check What You Know

What if a sales manager at an insurance company told you, "My sales reps don't know how to use the cold call list to obtain appointments. I think they need a training program—something to help them get more appointments out of the calls they make." What are some of the questions you'd ask?

____

____

____

____

As a trainer, you are more likely to be involved in the kind of focused needs assessment that takes place when someone has identified a real or perceived need for change. Because the scope of this type of needs assessment is limited to the issue at hand, it usually involves fewer people, takes less time, is less costly, and requires less expertise to conduct. But don't mistake "easier" for "less important." A thorough, carefully conducted needs assessment is essential to avoid wasting resources on unnecessary training or training that fails to achieve the desired results.

There can be many "triggers" for a focused needs assessment. Someone, like the Account Services CEO, has identified a real or apparent problem and makes an assumption that training is the way to solve it. The organization is introducing a new product or system, which means that people need to acquire new knowledge and/or skills. People are being hired or transferred into new jobs. A manager is looking for ways to make his team more productive or improve people's performance. Determining what role, if any, training has in addressing these kinds of issues or solving these kinds of problems starts with asking questions—lots and lots of questions.

Those questions include the following:

- *What change is needed?* What is the current situation and the desired situation or desired outcome? What is the gap between them? In the case of the sales reps at the insurance company, there appears to be a gap between the number of appointments that they should be making, compared to the number they are making now. But how many more appointments does the manager think that the reps should schedule?
- *What are all the possible causes for the gap between the current situation and the desired outcome?* Do people lack information? Do they lack skills? Do they need to change their attitudes? Do they lack motivation? Are there any procedural, operational, or organizational issues that might be causing the gap? What are the root causes? Perhaps the sales reps don't have all the skills they need to transform a cold call into an appointment. It's also possible that they are uncomfortable with the cold-calling process and don't think it's worth their time. In addition, the cold call lists themselves might include too many names of people who are not really viable prospects.
- *Why is it important to close the gap? What is likely to happen if nothing is done?* Sometimes a needs assessment makes it clear that it's not worth the cost of providing training or taking any other action to close a performance gap.

Perhaps the current situation is likely to change without any intervention, or maybe change isn't likely to make any meaningful difference to individuals or to the organization. For example, it might turn out that sales reps don't really need to learn how to make more appointments from the cold call lists because they have begun to use new, more effective methods for reaching prospects.

- *What are the possible ways to achieve the desired outcome?* Could a procedural change solve the problem? A staffing or organizational change? How difficult is it to learn what needs to be learned? Could structured on-the-job training and job aids accomplish the goals? Is training the best solution, or only one of several solutions? In the case of the sales reps, training might be one solution. But training won't do much good until the cold-call lists are updated with more viable prospects. After that's been done, the reps might benefit from training in cold calling techniques.
- *How urgent is the need?* Is there a specific time by which the performance gap needs to be closed? For example, if the company is planning to introduce a new product, it might be important to improve the sales reps' cold calling skills by the time that product is ready for the market.
- *Who are the stakeholders*—those who are interested in and affected by this situation and the desired outcomes? What are their levels of interest, knowledge, expertise, and points of view vis-à-vis this situation? Obviously, the sales manager who requested the training and is the primary decision-maker would be a key stakeholder. The sales reps themselves have an immediate interest in this situation, although they are likely to see it from a different perspective. The people who are responsible for putting together the cold call lists have an interest, as does the human resources department, which needs to be involved in any training efforts the company undertakes. And because the success of the sales staff affects the company's bottom line, the executive team has an interest in how the issue is addressed.
- *What are the constraints? What factors are likely to affect the ways in which the desired outcome is achieved?* The need to improve the sales reps' cold calling skills before a new product is introduced in a few weeks, along with a severely limited budget for training, would effectively rule out any type of training program that would take too much time and money to develop.
- *What are the characteristics of the target audience*—the people whose knowledge, skills, or attitudes need to change? Do they recognize the

need? Are they resistant to or amenable to change? What are their current levels of skill and knowledge? Their current attitudes? Their learning preferences? How large is the audience? Where are they located? How much time do they have available?

If the sales reps are frustrated by using outdated cold call lists, they might see little value in spending time learning to improve their cold-calling skills. Also, suppose that there are more than one hundred reps who are disbursed over a wide geographical area. In that case, bringing them together for training would be costly and time-consuming. Furthermore, if they have a wide range of skill level, from poor to very good, a one-size-fits-all training program is unlikely to achieve the desired results.

- *Who needs to be involved in the process of designing the training program?* Management? The learners? Instructional designers and materials developers? Other HR professionals? Subject-matter experts? It would be helpful to involve some of the sales reps themselves in the design process, along with their manager and an instructional design expert from HR and, perhaps, an expert in cold-calling skills. The executive team should also be kept informed and consulted at key checkpoints.

Key Questions for a Training Needs Assessment

- What is the gap between the current situation and the desired outcome?
- What are all the possible causes for the gap?
- Why is it important to close the gap?
- What are the possible ways to achieve the desired outcomes?
- How urgently does the gap need to be closed?
- Who are the stakeholders?
- What are the constraints?
- What are the characteristics of the target audience?
- Who needs to be involved in the training program design process?

2. Gathering Information

It's up to the trainer to do the detective work of uncovering the information needed to make a sound decision for improving performance through training. If someone has already done it, so much the better, but make sure you agree with the established need.

Tom W. Goad,
The First-Time Trainer

One of the primary reasons that organizations waste resources on training that isn't needed or doesn't achieve the desired outcome is that trainers make too many assumptions: After all, if the CEO, the human resources director, a division manager, or a team leader has requested training, there must be a real need, and training must be the way to meet it. Because they don't ask enough questions and accept what they are told without probing deeply enough, the information on which they base a training program may be incomplete or flawed. When that happens, organizations often invest in expensive training programs that fail to achieve any meaningful change.

Gathering information at the beginning of a training project is essential for determining whether training is really needed, but the process is helpful in other ways as well:

- Identifying and involving key stakeholders early in the process means that it is easier to gain their support and learn about any preferences and concerns they might have that could affect the way training is designed and delivered.
- An understanding of the "big picture" provides essential information about the context in which training will be conducted and a preview of some of the challenges that might come up during the design and development process.
- The initial research helps you become familiar with the content the training program needs to cover.
- Clarifying what the program is expected to achieve helps to establish the basis for evaluating the program's success.

Check What You Know

Which statements about gathering information are accurate?

1. ___ When interviewing people, it's a good idea to use leading questions to keep the discussion on the right track.
2. ___ Surveys and questionnaires provide the most useful information because they are the most objective.
3. ___ Although tests help you learn what people do and do not know, they do not usually provide much information about why a performance gap exists.
4. ___ The value of collecting information by observation is that you can compare what people really do to what they or others say they do.
5. ___ The key to a useful survey is including as many relevant questions as you can.

There are different ways to gather information about a potential training need. Some methods are more effective than others in gathering certain types of information. Some are very simple and inexpensive, while others, which may require special equipment or expertise, can be costly and time-consuming. Let's look briefly at the most common methods.

Interviews

Although interviews—in person, on the telephone, or in a virtual meeting space—take time to set up and conduct, they are worthwhile both in terms of the depth of information you can obtain and the opportunity to establish rapport with people who have an interest in the training. Interviewing different groups of people—those who requested the training, the participants' managers, the participants themselves, participants' co-workers, and/or direct reports, customers, subject-matter experts, and others—not only gives you more information than you would gather from only one individual or group, but it offers the different perspectives that help you figure out what's really going on. It's like looking at an elephant from different points of view—if all you could see was the trunk, you'd describe the animal as a very large nose, but if you saw only four legs, you'd say it was like a forest of thick tree trunks.

A patient, polite, thoughtful interview can help you uncover important information that no one would have thought to mention. Here are some guidelines:

- Once you've selected the interviewees, send an e-mail that explains your purpose, tells them how much time you'll need—usually twenty to thirty minutes—and asks for some times that would be convenient for them.
- Write out the initial questions you plan to ask. It's a good idea to send those questions ahead of time so the people you are interviewing can think about them.
- At the start of the interview, briefly clarify the purpose and give the person a chance to ask questions.
- Use open-ended questions (those that cannot be answered with "yes" or "no"). Let people talk, and listen carefully.
- Don't feel that you have to jump right in as soon as someone stops talking—a little silence often encourages people to add something they might not otherwise have thought to say.
- Be careful not ask "leading" questions, such as, "Don't you agree that most customer complaints are not justified?"
- To elicit more information, ask probing questions, such as, "Could you tell me more about . . . ?" or "Can you give me some examples of . . . ?"
- To help interviewees speak candidly, assure them that you will keep sensitive information confidential and the responses anonymous.
- Respect the value of people's time. Although it's helpful to take a minute or two to establish rapport at the beginning of an interview, avoid small talk or getting sidetracked onto issues that have nothing to do with the topic at hand.

Quick Quiz

If you were interviewing a manager to gather information about how well the team leaders in his department run meetings, which of the following would be useful questions?

1. ___ Are you happy with the way your team leaders run meetings?
2. ___ What, if anything, would you like team leaders to change about the way they run meetings? Why?
3. ___ Could you please describe the way that your team leaders run meetings?
4. ___ Do you have any team leaders who don't have a clue about how to run a meeting? Who are they?
5. ___ Do your team leaders need training on running meetings?

Asking Useful Questions

There are two primary types of questions: closed-ended and open-ended. Ask a close-ended question, and you can expect a "yes," "no," "maybe," a nod or shrug, or another one- or two-word answer: "It's red"; "fifteen or twenty." Open-ended questions, on the other hand, cannot be answered so simply, and for that reason they are far better at eliciting useful information. The table on the opposite page shows some examples.

Examples of Closed- and Open-Ended Questions

Closed-Ended Question	Open-Ended Question
Do your team members know how to delegate?	How well do your team members delegate? What are their strengths? Their challenges?
Could your team use a workshop in delegating skills?	What benefits do you think that improving team members' delegating skills might have for your team?
Do you enjoy delegating? Do you find it hard to delegate?	What about delegating do you enjoy the most? What do you find the most challenging?
Are there changes that your team members need to make in the way they delegate?	What changes do you think your team members need to make in the way they delegate?

Asking Follow-Up Questions

Follow-up questions help you clarify an interviewee's responses and probe for more information. They often help you uncover information that the person you are interviewing might not have thought to mention. the table gives some examples.

Samples of Follow-Up Questions

Initial Question	Follow-Up Questions
Please describe a change that you think team members need to make in the way they give feedback.	What are some reasons they need to make this change? What is likely to happen if they continue giving feedback the way they are giving it now?
What are some situations in which you find delegating to be challenging?	If I've got that right, you find delegating challenging when.... Please give me an example of a time that....

Focus Groups

Similar to a group interview, a focus group is a good way to explore the issues that triggered a training request and generate ideas for addressing them. When putting a focus group together, choose the participants carefully. Include key stakeholders along with others inside and outside of the organization who might have useful information, perspectives, and ideas. Prepare questions and distribute them to participants in advance, along with a statement of the reasons for the focus group and what the group will be trying to do. Facilitate focus groups carefully so that group members are encouraged to share ideas while keeping their attention on the issues at hand. Make sure that someone records the key points from the group's discussions.

Surveys and Questionnaires

Instruments that can easily be distributed online are helpful for gathering information and perspectives from large numbers of people and then comparing the responses to identify patterns. The key is making sure that the questions are clear and unambiguous, and that they are designed to elicit the information you are seeking. Giving people a choice of responses allows you to quantify the data, but always include space for open-ended comments. Keep in mind that people are busy, so limit the number of questions you ask.

When sending out a survey or questionnaire, include a brief introduction that explains the purpose of the questions, how you will use the information, and, if possible, how answering these questions will benefit the respondents. Include a deadline for responding.

A common problem with questionnaires and surveys is that only a few people are likely to complete them by the deadline. You might need to send a reminder, or two, to prompt the others, emphasizing the importance of their responses. I've also known people who have given rewards—a card for a cup of coffee, an entry into a drawing for a prize, or a small gift to charity in their name—to increase the number of responses.

If your organization does not have software for conducting online surveys, there are several web-based services, such as SurveyMonkey, that you can use to conduct a survey for little or no cost.

Tests

A test can give you a pretty good idea of how much people already know about something or how well they are able to carry out a procedure. Tests can provide factual data that helps you zero in on the gap between what people already know or are able to do, and what they need to know and are able to do. But use tests with caution. For results to be valid, tests need to be carefully designed and administered. And they rarely provide information that helps you discover *why* a performance gap exists and evaluate the importance of bringing about change.

Assessments

An assessment can be a good way to measure people's attitudes and personal characteristics. The information can be used to design the program so that it meets individual needs, and the assessment results can be incorporated into the training itself. For example, people might use the results of an assessment of their leadership strengths and challenges or the ways in which their personality styles affect their communication with others to come up with improvement strategies. Like tests, assessments need to be carefully designed and administered to be of value.

Observation

One excellent way to discover a performance or knowledge gap is to watch people do a job and/or to observe the results of the work they do. You can watch and listen to the way a loan processor explains options to a customer and/or examine the accuracy of the documents the processor completes. Sometimes observation will uncover a process or procedural issue that no one has recognized—people might be making errors because they do not have access to correct information or because they do not have enough time to do a job correctly.

Observations are also useful for comparing what people say with what they or others actually do. The customer service manager might say that the representatives need a workshop to learn how to ask questions when taking orders, but your observation shows that they know how to ask questions—what they need is a job aid to remind them of what questions to ask in specific situations.

Like interviews, observations take time. Observers need to know what they are looking for and how to avoid preconceptions that could blind them to what is really going on. They need to be as non-intrusive as possible, both to avoid interfering with—and possibly changing—the behavior and to keep from making the person being observed uncomfortable.

How to Start Collecting Information

It can be hard to know how to start gathering information. If you just ask questions haphazardly or ask questions of the wrong people, you might end up wasting everybody's time without finding out what you need to know. Here are some steps you can take to start and keep going in a productive direction:

1. Begin by listing the initial questions you think need to be answered. Ask yourself: What do you know? What do you not know?
2. Determine what you will do to find answers to those initial questions—who you will ask and what methodology you will use.
3. Once you've asked the first round of questions, step back and review the information. Ask yourself once again: What do you know? What do you not know? Make another list of questions and do another round. Keep going until you seem to have enough information to move ahead.

See the table below for an outline of the methods described above and what to consider for each.

Methods for Gathering Information

Method	To Consider
Interviews—in person, by telephone, in virtual meeting space	Take time to set up and conduct
	Can provide depth of information
	Offer chance to establish rapport with stakeholders
	Provide a variety of perspectives
	Need to be planned
	Work best with open-ended and probing questions

Method	To Consider
Focus groups	Help people talk about issues that triggered a training request and generate ideas for addressing them Participants must be carefully chosen Useful to prepare and distribute questions in advance Must be facilitated carefully
Surveys and questionnaires	Way to get information and perspectives from large numbers of people Can compare responses to identify patterns Questions must be clear, unambiguous, and designed to elicit specific information Can be difficult to collect everyone's responses
Tests	Can provide factual data about what people already know or are able to do Can provide a clear baseline for measuring training success Tests need to be carefully designed Not everything can be tested
Assessments	Can help measure people's attitudes, behavior, and personal characteristics Can provide a baseline for measuring training success Must be carefully designed and administered to be of value
Observation	Excellent way to discover a performance or knowledge gap, uncover its root causes, and compare what people say with what they or others actually do Time-consuming and labor-intensive Requires patience and expertise in observation skills Requires observing several people in order to identify patterns of behavior

Sources of Information

To gather the right information during a needs assessment, you must determine where you are most likely to find it. Sources might include the following:

- The learners—the audience for training
- The learners' managers
- Human resources
- The learners' co-workers
- Internal and external customers
- Subject-matter experts
- Vendors
- Competitors
- Industry experts
- Performance reports
- Job descriptions
- Statistical reports and other relevant documents
- Policy and procedures manuals
- Competency lists

What's a Task Analysis?

An important part of the training program design process is learning exactly how a job or a task is supposed to be done and what skills and knowledge people need to do it. That's accomplished by performing a task analysis (also called a job analysis).

The objective of a task analysis is to break a task or job down into its component parts and identify the actions needed to complete it properly. For example, if you were designing a program to help team leaders run more productive meetings, you would do a task analysis to identify the specific tasks involved. For each of the tasks, you could then identify the skills and knowledge the team leaders would need.

Task: Prepare an agenda.

The steps include:

- Collecting the topics to address during the meeting
- Organizing the topics into a logical order
- Estimating the time needed for each topic
- [etc.]

What team leaders need to know and be able to do:

- The components of an agenda
- The purpose of an agenda
- What an agenda should look like
- Where to gather information
- How to organize topics
- How to estimate time
- [etc.]

There are various methods for conducting a task analysis: interview people who do the task or job; interview people who know how the task or job is supposed to be done; and/or observe people who are actually doing the work. There are advantages and disadvantages to each method, so it's usually best to use them in combination.

Conducting task and job analyses requires excellent observation and interviewing skills. You need to keep in mind that the goal is to learn the *right* way of doing something. That means making sure the people you observe or interview are doing the job the way it is supposed to be done. Otherwise, you might develop an entire training program in which people learn to do things the wrong way.

Boris and Marietta's Progress

Boris and Marietta did several things to gather information:

- Interviewed the CEO to learn more about what she thought needed to be changed. Among other things, they learned that a client had recently complained about an e-mail with confidential financial information that was sent to a group.
- Met with several teams to discuss their use of e-mail. People agreed that e-mail was essential to their business—"I don't know what we did without it"—but that unnecessary and confusing messages were also wasting a lot of their time.
- Reviewed more than one hundred randomly selected internal and external e-mail messages, which confirmed what they had already learned: people were writing too many unnecessary messages and sending too many "group" e-mails; the writing was often unclear, disorganized, and confusing; many of the messages to clients were sloppy, with spelling and grammatical errors; and some messages addressed sensitive subjects, contained confidential information, or included content that could be considered inappropriate or offensive.
- Sent out a survey to learn more about people's perceptions of their own and others' e-mail use. The results indicated that many employees felt that e-mail took up too much of their time. Interestingly, most respondents rated their own use of e-mail satisfactory or better, while indicating that other people needed to send fewer e-mail messages and write more clearly.

3. Analyzing the Information

. . . begin with the end in mind and keep it in the forefront of your thinking the entire time.

Jean Marrapodi, "Never Lose Sight of Your Audience," in T.L. Gargiulo, A.M. Pangarkar, and T. Kirkwood (Eds.), *The Trainer's Portable Mentor*

A thorough needs assessment may result in an overwhelming amount of information. Not all of it will be useful, but before you can determine what to keep and what to throw out, you need to figure out what it all means. It's like sitting down with a box that's filled with puzzle pieces. There's a pretty complete puzzle in there somewhere, but to find the right pieces and fit them together, you first have to dump them all out onto a table top. If the puzzle isn't too complicated, a clear picture might emerge quickly, but if there are hundreds of tiny pieces, it takes a while, and there will be lots of false starts. And sometimes you'll need to stop in the middle to track down pieces that have found their way under the sofa.

Once you think that you finally have a pretty clear picture of the situation, the next step is to examine everything to clarify and confirm the original assumptions that change is needed and training is the way to achieve that change.

At the beginning of this chapter, you saw the key questions that the analysis is intended to answer. Now let's look at them more closely.

What Change Is Needed?

As you learned earlier, the original idea that triggers the training program design process is often vague and incomplete—"I'd like to do something about my tennis game" or "We need to do something about the way customer complaints are being handled." It's like saying, "I'd like to go on a vacation." The idea is great—but what's the destination? Without knowing where you intend to go, you can't figure out the best way to get there.

One of the most important tasks in the analysis stage of ADDIE is to figure out exactly what needs to change and come up with a concrete description of the expected outcome: I'd like to spend a week hiking in the Sierras; I'd like to improve my tennis game enough so I can complete in the WTA tournament next spring; we'd like to respond to 80 percent of customer complaints within twenty-four hours. Once you have clarified that outcome, keep it firmly in mind—it will help you stay on track.

How Urgent or Important Is It to Change the Current Situation?

There are lots of things that would be nice to have but aren't really essential. I'd like to buy a new car because my old one doesn't have GPS or a backup camera, but it's hard to justify the expenditure because it runs just fine. But if it kept stalling when I stopped at a light or I discovered that the engine needed to be replaced, I'd have a very good reason to buy a new one.

Organizations sometimes spend a great deal of time and money on a training program without asking an essential question: "What is likely to happen if we do nothing—if we leave things as they are?" Like my idea for a new car, change might be nice to have, but is it urgent? Is it worth the investment?

That question might be easy to answer: the result of doing nothing might be an unacceptably high level of production errors, accidents, or lost customers; lowered morale that could reduce productivity and increase turnover; or an inability for people to do their jobs. Training might be urgent because new regulations are being introduced, a new product is about to be launched, or a new system is being installed.

Identifying Priorities

You might already be familiar with Steven Covey's matrix for identifying priorities. Considering a training need in terms of the four quadrants in the table below can help you determine whether it's a priority or even whether it should be addressed at all.

Steven Covey's Matrix

	Urgent	**Not Urgent**
Important	*1* There are too many serious accidents; a new product is about to be launched; the company is facing lawsuits; new hires need to know how to do their jobs	*2* There are too many unnecessary meetings; managers' reports are difficult to read; employees are not using time as productively as they could
Not Important	*3* In a company that's about to be reorganized, some teams are not meeting deadlines	*4* Making minor wording changes in a document that has already been edited, proofread, and approved

THINK ABOUT IT

In which of the following situations is change "nice-to-have"? In which is change important but not urgent? In which is change important and urgent?

N — Nice to have
I = Important but not urgent
UI = Urgent and important

1. ___ Significant changes in governmental regulations that affect the way in which loan applications are processed will take place in three months.
2. ___ Sales assistants have expressed interest in learning how to use PowerPoint to make presentations so that they can take on new responsibilities.
3. ___ During the past six months, an increasing number of top performers have left the company for competing organizations, and their exit interviews indicated that nearly 25 per cent were unhappy with their relationships with their managers.
4. ___ Customers have been complaining that they have to wait on the phone for long periods before they can reach a support person with a problem or question.

It would be both urgent and important for people involved in processing loan applications to know about impending changes in government regulations so that they are ready to conform to those regulations as soon as they take effect. It would be nice for sales assistants to learn to use PowerPoint so they can take on new responsibilities, but unless there is a business requirement for them to do so, it's neither urgent nor very important. If top performers are leaving because they are unhappy with their managers, it's both urgent and important to address the situation because the company cannot achieve its strategic goals without its best performers. Customer complaints about long wait periods need to be addressed, but unless the situation is leading to an immediate loss of customers, change is important but not necessarily urgent.

What Are the Reasons for the Gap Between the Current Situation and the Desired Outcome? Is Training the Best Way to Close It?

Instructional designers need to recognize that the desire for change that sparked the idea for training—people are making mistakes, productivity is dropping, customers are being offended, team members are not meeting deadlines, top performers are leaving to work for the competitor—is seldom the whole story. In many instances, it's only a symptom of the root cause, or causes, of the situation. Workers might be ignoring safety procedures not because they fail to understand the procedures or their importance, but because they don't have the right equipment or because their supervisors discourage them from taking the extra time. Sales staff in the field might not be completing customer contact reports correctly because they don't have the newest version of the software. Late-night help-desk staff might be rude and abrupt to callers because there are too few people on their shift to keep up with the calls. Top performers might be taking jobs with the competitor because they are being expected to work unreasonably long hours. Uncovering the root cause or causes for a situation is essential before deciding what role, if any, training can play in effecting change.

Check What You Know

For each of the situations below, list some possible reasons for the performance gap and think about some of the ways, other than training, to effect change in these situations:

1. Company policy is that all the managers do a formal performance appraisal for each of their employees at least once a year. Nearly 35 percent of the managers are doing the appraisals late, doing them incorrectly, or not doing them at all.
   Possible reasons for gap:

   ____

   ____

Ways other than training to effect change:

---

2. A hospital that serves a large population without health insurance has emergency room wait times of up to twelve hours. The new director wants to cut the maximum wait time in half by the end of the year. Possible reasons for gap:

   Ways other than training to effect change:

   ---

3. A nonprofit legal clinic offers free or low-cost advice to people whose income falls below a certain level. To use the attorneys' time most efficiently, the clinic uses volunteers who screen clients to make sure they qualify for services and gather information about their need for legal services by asking a series of questions. The clinic manager has noticed that the volunteers, who sign up for three-hour shifts once a week, often sit around with nothing to do.
   Possible reasons for gap:

   Ways other than training to effect change:

Reasons That Training Might Not Be the Answer

Although training might at first appear to be the best way to address a performance gap, a closer look might reveal that training, or training alone, is unlikely to solve the problem. Here are examples of situations in which something other than training might be needed:

- There is an operational, procedural, or systems problem.
- People are not well suited to their jobs.
- People do not have enough time, information, equipment, or other resources.
- People are not motivated to improve performance.
- Managers are not clearly communicating expectations or do not know how to coach employees (that situation might indicate that the managers need training).

4. Consider the Stakeholders

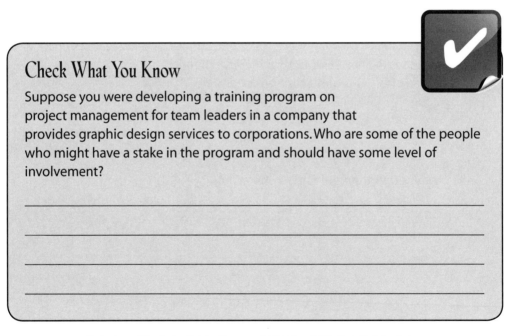

Check What You Know

Suppose you were developing a training program on project management for team leaders in a company that provides graphic design services to corporations. Who are some of the people who might have a stake in the program and should have some level of involvement?

____

____

____

____

Change initiatives such as training do not happen in a vacuum. They need the support of various people within—and possibly outside of—the organization. An important part of the needs assessment process is identifying the people who have a stake in changing the situation so that those people can be brought into the process in some way.

Stakeholders can include:

- *Decision-makers*. The people who decide what types of initiatives to undertake and how to allocate resources are among the key stakeholders for any training program. Depending on the situation, they may be concerned only with the bottom line—they want assurance that the training is worth the investment—or they might have strong ideas about the type of program that is developed. Decision-makers can include your manager and the manager who has requested training all the way up to the executive team, the CEO, or in some cases, a board of directors. In some instances, they may include others, such as clients or customers, who have a say in what training is done and how training is delivered. The more you know about the decision-makers' interests and concerns, the more able you will be to gain their support.
- *People who are directly affected by the situation*. When meetings are poorly run, everyone who attends them has an interest in seeing them improved. Managers who base decisions and actions on data provided by others have a stake in making sure that the data they receive is accurate and in a usable form. Employees who care about their job performance have a stake in their managers' ability to communicate expectations clearly and provide support and feedback while they work. People who need assistance, collaboration, and cooperation from colleagues to carry out their job responsibilities have a stake in improving relationships within and outside of their departments. Executives who are concerned about retaining top performers have a stake in helping employees achieve their career goals within the organization. Both internal and external customers have a stake in efforts that will improve responses to their needs and concerns. All those people are invaluable sources of the information you need to design and develop the program; they may also have differing needs and perspectives that must be considered for the training to succeed.

- *Subject-matter experts*. One of the things I like best about training is learning new things. Through the programs I've designed and developed, I've learned about the art of leadership; how to manage teams, delegate, and manage my priorities; and much, much more. Much of what I learned was by working with people who were experts in the subject matter, people who had the information and best practices that formed the content of my programs. Those kinds of subject-matter experts—experienced, skilled people within or outside of your organization—are invaluable resources. But they are nearly always very busy people, and to get their full support, respect their time, make sure they know why the program is important, and let them know that you value their contributions.
- *The learners*. Among the most important stakeholders are the people whose skills, knowledge, and/or attitudes need to change as a result of training. You'll need to know a great deal about the audience in order to make decisions throughout the design and development process. In some cases, you will know or be able to meet some of the people who will participate in the training, but in others, you will only be able to learn their characteristics, because individual learners have not yet been identified or they are not available for one reason or another. But the more you know about the audience and the more you are actually able to involve the learners in the design and development process, the greater the likelihood of success. (See below for more on the questions to ask about the learners.)

5. Consider the Learners

Never lose sight of your audience or their goals.
The rest almost takes care of itself.

Jean Marrapodi, "Never Lose Sight of Your Audience," in T.L. Gargiulo, A.M. Pangarkar, and T. Kirkwood (Eds.), *The Trainer's Portable Mentor*

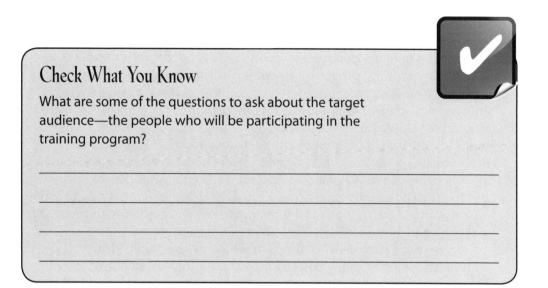

Check What You Know

What are some of the questions to ask about the target audience—the people who will be participating in the training program?

____

____

____

____

Before investing the time and money to develop a new product, a company does market research to identify potential purchasers and learn as much as possible about them. What they learn may significantly affect the product design. The original idea may be tweaked or radically changed to make it more attractive to customers—the product might be made larger or smaller, less expensive, brighter in color, easier to use, more durable. The more thorough the market research—the more the company can learn about what customers want and need—the greater their chance of making a profit.

Surprisingly, organizations sometimes go about the process of designing and developing training programs without ever stopping to focus on their primary customers—the learners who comprise the target audience. Yet the purpose of training is to bring about change in the learners' knowledge, skills, and/or attitudes. To design a program that accomplishes that goal, you need to find out as much as you can about them.

- *Who are the learners? What jobs do they do? What's their relationship to one another?* Some training programs are intended for a specific group of people—telephone skills for newly hired customer service representatives, safety regulations for line supervisors in a manufacturing plant, report writing for bank auditors. When the audience is limited in that way, it's relatively easy to learn a lot about the learners, such as the details of the kinds of work they do, their prior experiences with and preferences for training, and the kinds of time they have available. You'll use that information to focus training as closely as possible on their needs.

But many training programs are intended for a broader audience. For example, a workshop on interpersonal communication, business writing, or time management might draw a wide mix of people from all areas and all levels of an organization. The program might include managers and line staff; people from marketing, manufacturing, and the legal department; in some cases, even customers or vendors. And many training programs include people from different organizations. When the audience is broad and likely to be mixed, you will need to do some research to find out who is likely to take the training and what kinds of jobs they do so that you can make informed assumptions to guide the design process.

For programs such as workshops in which people will be learning with others, it's also important to know such things as whether they are strangers or close colleagues, and whether managers and their direct reports will be participating at the same time. For example, strangers might need more time to connect with one another, and people who are in the same workshop as their managers might not feel like engaging in certain kinds of activities or exploring certain topics.

- *How large is the target audience? Where are the learners located? What kind of time do they have available for training?* The size and location of the audience affects decisions about the training program in several ways. The larger the audience, the less the per-person cost of development: an e-learning program, for example, might not provide a good return on investment for a small group of learners, but it might be a very good investment if the audience numbers in the hundreds. The location of learners might determine whether training can be provided in a live, in-person workshop. If they are widely disbursed, it might be too costly or impractical to bring them together in a central location, so a virtual workshop might be a good alternative. If learners work different shifts or can't be spared from their jobs for more than an hour or two at a time, training might need to be provided in a self-study format or in a sequence of short modules.
- *Why will people take this training? What do they know about why the program is being held?* Adults want to know why they are learning, and in particular, how the learning will benefit them. Some of the first questions to ask when designing a program are, "Why will people take this program? How does

this training relate to their jobs? In what ways will this learning benefit them? Are they a self-selecting group who will sign up for training on their own? Is the training required? Will their managers "encourage" them to participate? It's also helpful to think about what the learners have in common vis-à-vis the subject, especially when the target audience is very broad. All that information keeps you focused on the learners, helping you shape the program to meet their needs.

- *What do learners already know/what are they able to do? What do they need to know/be able to do?* Adults learn best when they can relate what they learn to what they already know and to their existing skill sets. An understanding of the learners' existing knowledge and skills is the starting point for identifying the skills, knowledge, and competencies they need to achieve the desired outcome of the program and for finding ways to build on that foundation to help them learn.

  An activity that I've found helpful is to stand in front of a whiteboard or flip-chart page, or to open a blank document on my computer, and list everything I've been able to learn about the knowledge, skills, and attitudes that learners are likely to bring with them to training. This exercise helps me determine whether I know enough about them or need to do more research. It also helps me recognize diversity of experience, skills, and knowledge among the audience that I need to consider when designing the program. For example, I may need to decide whether to establish prerequisites for training or come up with a way to provide certain learners with knowledge or skills that most of the others already have. The table below is an example of this kind of list.

Assessing What Learners Know/Are Able to Do and Need to Know/Be Able to Do

Topic of training: Changing a tire

Learners Already Know/Are Able to Do	Learners Need to Know/Be Able to Do
How to recognize a flat tire	Decide which tools to use
Why a tire needs to be changed	Take the tire off the rim
Where to find the spare [some learners]	Remove the spare from the storage compartment
Where to find the tool box [some learners]	Put the spare on the rim
Etc.	Etc.

- *What previous experience have learners had with training? What preferences do they have?* I used to conduct workshops for correctional officers and sheriffs' deputies who worked in the jails. They would often arrive at the workshop armed with newspapers and magazines to get them through the day. I did what I could to engage them, but it wasn't much use. After this had happened two or three times, I told one group how frustrated I felt and asked for their help. Most of them barely looked up. but a few kind souls finally filled me in. "We haven't got any say about whether to come to these workshops," one deputy said. "They tell us to come, we come. Forty hours a year, required. Waste of time, no offense intended."

Not only were the workshops mandated, I learned, but the deputies' experiences with training—a series of boring, trainer-focused workshops on subjects that had no apparent relevance to their jobs—had created the expectation that it was something to be endured.

From then on, I started every workshop with activities that involved the deputies right away and helped them discover the ways in which the training would benefit them in their jobs. It didn't succeed with everyone—there were always a few who dozed straight through or hung out at the back of the room with their newspapers—but comments that the deputies made as they left the room and on their evaluation forms indicated

Questions to Ask About Learners

- Who are the learners and what jobs do they do?
- How large is the audience?
- Where are learners located? Are they in the same location?
- What kind of time do learners have available for training?
- Are they self-selecting or is this training mandated?
- What do learners know about why this training is being held?
- What do learners already know or what are they already able to do?
- What do they need to know or be able to do as a result of training?
- What previous experiences have learners had with training? How do they prefer to learn?
- Do learners know one another? Are they from the same or different areas of the organization? From different organizations?
- Are learners at the same level of the organization?
- Will managers and their direct reports be taking the same training, at the same time?

that most of them found the workshops far more interesting and useful than had earlier groups.

Gathering information about the learners' experiences with training and the types of training they prefer isn't always easy, especially if the audience is large and diverse. But dig around: you might discover, as I did, that the people who are likely to participate in this program have complained in the past about training that was boring, didn't seem relevant to their work, or was too "touchy-feely"; you might learn that they prefer training delivered in short "bursts" so they don't have to leave their work for an entire day, or that they do best with self-directed learning that they can do at their own pace and on their own time. Whatever information you can find about the learners' training experiences and preferences will be useful when you consider what kind of program is most likely to meet their needs.

6. Identifying Constraints and Other Factors That Impact the Training Program Design

THINK ABOUT IT

What are some of the constraints and other factors that might limit your options or otherwise affect the choices you make when designing a training program?

____

____

____

____

Whether it's taking a trip, remodeling your home, starting a business, or launching a new product, it would be nice to have unlimited resources and be able to do everything exactly the way that you wanted to do it. But for any of your projects to succeed, you need to temper your vision with reality. For training projects, you need to consider—and keep firmly in mind—the following:

- *The time you have available*. The people who request training may have little understanding of the time it takes to plan and develop a program. Even instructional designers with years of experience can easily underestimate how long the process will take. But when you try to squeeze a lengthy planning and development process into a limited amount of time, the result is that key steps are skipped, mistakes are made, and the program doesn't quite meet expectations.

  Be realistic about what you can reasonably do in the amount of time that you and other people who will be involved in the program design and development process have available. Think about everything that has to be done before the program will be ready to launch, and add some extra time for the unexpected delays and problems that are sure to come up. If you have a limited amount of time, limit the type and scope of program to what can reasonably be developed within the time constraints. That might mean revisiting the original idea and desired outcomes. It's far better to trim back what you hope to achieve than to try to do too much in too little time.

- *The budget*. When training projects are done in a haphazard way, it's easy for costs to balloon out of control. But as organizations become more and more cost-conscious, budgets for everything are under increasing scrutiny. Everyone has to do more with less, and training is no exception. As an instructional designer, you'll be expected to use budget dollars wisely. That means clarifying the budget before designing the program so you can plan carefully and make thoughtful choices about everything from delivery methods to media and materials.

- *Expertise*. You might know how to change a tire, but if your car's engine conks out, you would probably take the car to a skilled mechanic. Many instructional designers know how to put together a workshop, but not all of them have the skills to develop e-learning or the technical knowledge to run a virtual web-based workshop. Be realistic about what you and your team are able to do, unless you have the budget to bring in experts with the knowledge and skills you lack.

- *Politics and culture*. Sometimes there are real political or cultural issues that impact the choices made during the design and development process. A key stakeholder might insist on an e-learning program when you believe that a workshop would be a less costly and just as satisfactory a way to effect change. An organizational value for collaboration and cooperation might lead to a preference for a workshop over self-directed learning, even for subjects that really do not benefit from interaction between learners. Those kinds of issues can create challenges for instructional designers whose goal is to provide the best training possible and make the best use of the organization's investment, but it's important to recognize and consider them throughout the process. If you believe that a political or cultural issue creates a real obstacle to providing training that achieves the desired outcome, you may need to build a case for proceeding in a different way. There is nothing to be gained for you or for the stakeholders by remaining silent.

7. Determine Who Should Be Involved in Designing the Training Program

We would get very little work done and achieve very few of our objectives without involving other people. Politicians need the ideas, expertise, and support of a great many people with a diverse range of talents and points of view to plan and run a successful campaign. Architects need the participation of clients, colleagues, artists, engineers, contractors, government officials, and, sometimes, the general public, to move from idea to completed building. In the same way, instructional designers need to involve a variety of people in the process of designing, developing, implementing, and evaluating a successful training program.

You've already learned about the importance of involving key stakeholders as early in the process as possible. Some of those stakeholders may be actively involved as you move forward, while others will remain on the periphery, becoming involved only when important decisions need to be made. Others, such as writers and subject-matter experts, will move in and out as their skills and expertise are needed, just as electricians and plumbers come into a construction process at certain stages of the project.

At this point, you might not be able to identify everyone who will need to be involved in the development and implementation process. But before starting the program design, enlist the help and support of everyone who needs to be involved in developing the learning objectives that will form the foundation of the training program and in determining the way in which training will be delivered. (You'll learn more about identifying the learning objectives and selecting delivery methods later in this book.)

How to Involve Others

The relationships that you establish with stakeholders and others at the beginning and throughout the design and development process can significantly affect the success of the training program. Here are some suggestions for involving people in ways that encourage their support and collaboration:

- As mentioned earlier, involve key stakeholders early in the process. Elicit their ideas and help them feel that they are an integral part of the process, not outsiders. Make sure that decision-makers and those with essential knowledge or skills will be available when you need them.
- Help everyone who is involved in the program understand why it is being undertaken, what it will achieve, why it is important, and how their contributions will help it succeed. Let people know that you recognize and respect their knowledge and expertise.
- Clearly communicate your expectations. Make sure that people know exactly what you need from them, why you need it, and when you need it. Ask them to let you know as soon as possible if they will be unable to provide something you need.
- Respect people's schedules and priorities. Keep in mind that people are busy, and don't expect them to put your training project ahead of the things they consider more important. Instead of giving people deadlines, tell them what you need and ask when they can get it to you. Let them know that you appreciate their help.

8. Design It or Buy It?

A writer friend with two pre-teen daughters recently gave up the little room she'd been using as a studio so that each of her girls could have her own bedroom. Admirable, I thought, but she can't afford to build an addition to her house or rent an office, so where will she work? She was way ahead of me:

she bought a prefabricated room that a contractor friend is going to erect in her back yard—an instant studio, for a fraction of the cost of building one from scratch.

It's also not always necessary to design and develop a training program from scratch. There is a huge supply of "prefabricated," or "off-the-shelf," programs to choose from, on a wide range of topics such as leadership skills, running productive meetings, delegating, using PowerPoint and Excel, basic bookkeeping and accounting . . . the list goes on and on. Some programs are ready to use as is, and others can be easily customized to meet specific needs. But using an off-the-shelf program is not always the best way to save time and money, and there is a lot to consider when selecting the right program to meet your learners' needs.

Types of Off-the-Shelf Programs

Off-the-shelf training programs range from public workshops and web-based seminars to computer-based tutorials and self-study workbooks. Here's an overview:

- *Public workshops.* Universities and colleges, professional associations, and private companies offer a wide range of workshops that are open to the public and/or to association members. Many of these workshops are on generic soft-skill topics that are of interest to a wide audience—communication skills, delegating, meeting planning, time management, leadership, and the like. But many of them focus on specific topics of interest to specific audiences—examples from a quick web search include finance for non-financial executives, human resources and the law for health professionals, inventory management techniques, and report writing for environmental engineers.
- *Customized in-house workshops.* Many of the same organizations that provide public workshops will provide a version of the training that is customized to meet the needs of your organization and your learners. The degree of customization varies from minor tweaking to a complete overhaul of the design and content.
- *e-Learning programs.* If you decide that e-learning is the best delivery method for the situation, look at what's out there before developing your own. There are lots of good e-learning programs available on a wide range of topics, some of which come on CD-ROM, some of which

can be downloaded from a website, and some of which are taken online. Although many of these programs are expensive, some are free of charge and others may be available for a nominal fee.

- *Public web-based workshops and seminars.* My daily e-mail usually includes at least a couple of offers from associations or private companies to attend a web event of some kind. They include live workshops in which I can participate and taped presentations that I can view whenever I choose. Like e-learning programs, some of these "webinars" are available free of charge or for a nominal fee, and some cost several hundred dollars.
- *Self-paced print programs.* Even in this highly technological age, the self-paced learning program in the form of a workbook is still alive and well. Professional organizations, universities, publishers, and private companies offer self-study workbooks on a wide range of topics. Although these training programs are designed for people to take on their own, the venders often sell or provide trainer guides so the materials can be used for workshops or other group training. Many of the programs are now accompanied by CDs and/or online support.
- *Prepackaged workshops.* These "takeout" packages include everything that trainers need to conduct a workshop: a trainer's guide, participant handouts, a slide presentation, activities, and supplementary materials and information. The package can be used as is or adapted to meet specific needs. See the Resources section at the back of the book for descriptions of a few ready-to-go training packages.

Finding Off-the-Shelf Programs

Enter the topic of your program into a search engine and you might find hundreds of possibilities. Some will be from professional associations such as ASTD and the American Management Association, others from publishers such as Pfeiffer or HRD Press, others through universities, and many from private companies that specialize in off-the-shelf training. You can usually find a detailed description of specific programs on the organization's website, including learning objectives, agenda or content overview, methodology, delivery system—and, of course, price.

Other training professionals are also a good source of information about off-the-shelf programs. Let people know what you are looking for, and ask for suggestions about programs they've used or participated in. Your own organization might even have a supply of programs that they have purchased or developed that could be used as is or adapted for the current need.

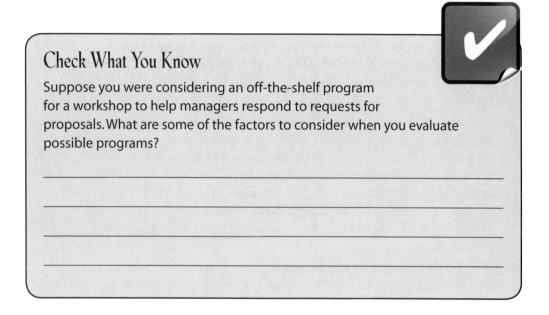

Check What You Know

Suppose you were considering an off-the-shelf program for a workshop to help managers respond to requests for proposals. What are some of the factors to consider when you evaluate possible programs?

____

____

____

____

Evaluating Off-the-Shelf Programs

The right off-the-shelf program can save a significant amount of time and money. It can also provide a level of expertise in content and instructional design that is unavailable in your organization. But any program is worth the investment only if it meets your learners' needs or can be adapted in a cost-effective way.

Key factors to consider when you're trying to decide whether to use an off-the-shelf program instead of developing one from scratch include the following:

- *Cost*. There can be a significant difference between the costs of similar off-the-shelf programs, so it's worth shopping around. But think about more than the initial cost: consider any costs involved in adapting the program to meet your organization's needs. A more expensive program might be the better buy if it requires less customization or can be customized more easily.

- *Adaptability*. Many off-the-shelf programs, including public workshops or webinars, printed self-study workbooks, and most e-learning programs, have little or no flexibility. Even prepackaged workshops might be difficult to customize because of technical limitations or copyright issues. That doesn't matter if the program is a perfect fit with your needs—but few programs are. Unless the existing program closely fits your needs, you might do better to find a program that can be easily adapted for your situation.
- *Licensing and certification requirements*. Some off-the-shelf programs restrict use in some way. You might be required to sign up a certain number of people or to buy a certain number of workbooks or assessment instruments. The program might need to be used within a certain amount of time. As mentioned above, you might need to agree not to make any changes. For some programs, you might be required to be trained by one of the vender's trainers or those who have been through a certification process.
- *Quality*. The quality of off-the-shelf programs ranges from superb to extremely poor. An excellent program might be far superior than anything you would be able to develop in-house; a poor one is not only a waste of money, but it can lead to frustration and negative feelings about training. Buy only from reputable organizations, and carefully check out any program that you are considering. Talk to people who've used and taken the program. If it's a public workshop and you are considering using it for large numbers of people in your organization, attend a session.

Other Factors to Consider

I'm a fan of carefully selected off-the-shelf training programs, especially for small organizations with limited resources. (Disclaimer: I ran a training company for many years that provided customized in-house workshops and self-study workbooks on business writing.) But in my work as a training consultant, I have watched companies spend too much money on programs that never left the shelf because they didn't really fit anyone's needs; I have also watched companies struggle to customize programs that would have been far easier to develop from scratch. From those experiences and the experiences of other training professionals, here are some suggestions for making the best use of off-the-shelf training.

- *Buy a program only if you need it.* Just because a program looks interesting doesn't mean that your organization will necessarily have a use for it. Wait until you've identified a need before you buy. If it's a good program, it will still be there when you need it.
- *Buy a program only if it has a good chance of working.* Unless it's very cheap and there are no copyright issues, avoid the temptation to buy a program that really doesn't fit your needs with the vague idea of cannibalizing it for your own purposes. If you're just looking for ideas, do a web search: you'll probably come up with lots of ideas you can use to develop a program of your own. (But be careful to respect copyrights.)
- *Make sure the program is sound.* Evaluate any program you are considering from an instructional point of view. Does it reflect adult learning principles? Do the content, activities, and structure support the learning objectives? Is the content valid?
- *Find out whether the program can be customized.* As mentioned above, some programs can be customized for your organization and group, and some cannot. If the program really does fit your needs without customization, fine. If not, learn what would be involved in customizing it—including the cost, time, and who would do the work, you or the vender.
- *Talk to people who have used the program.* Seek out others who have used the program to meet similar training needs and ask how well it worked for them. Probe for specifics about how well the program worked with different learners in different situations. Ask about any problems they may have had with the program or with the vender.
- *Make sure you know what the purchase price includes.* Some venders give away the facilitator's guide for a workshop but charge a minimum fee for the participant workbooks, videos, or other materials you need to run it. Some sell only limited rights to use the program. To avoid surprises, ask the vender for a written description of exactly what and what is not included in the price.

Boris and Marietta's Progress

The results of Boris and Marietta's initial research made it clear that change was needed. But was training the solution? Here's a summary of their conclusions:

- They agreed that the CEO's original assumption was true—the ways in which people were using e-mail needed to be changed. There was an abundance of unnecessary e-mail, confusing "stream of consciousness" messages, and e-mail with inappropriate content. Poor e-mail use was affecting productivity and putting the organization at risk of lawsuits. Although the situation wasn't urgent, it was of high priority. The longer it took to bring about change, the more mistakes would be made, the more time would be wasted, and the greater the risk of a lawsuit.
- They found three primary reasons for the problems with e-mail:
  - *Lack of information.* Although someone in the legal department had written e-mail policies several months ago, they had never been distributed and only a few people even knew they existed.
  - *Lack of skills.* A significant number of people needed to improve their business writing skills.
  - *Lack of understanding.* Nearly everyone thought that e-mail was a problem, but few people understood how their own use of e-mail contributed to the problem and how important proper, productive use of e-mail was to the business.
- They concluded that training would be one way to improve the quality of the e-mail employees sent and reduce unproductive time spent on e-mail, but that it would be both unnecessary and unrealistic to put everyone in the company through an e-mail workshop. They would recommend that the company distribute the written policies and encourage teams to use them to develop guidelines for e-mail use. Training could be used to reinforce and support that effort.

- They identified three key stakeholders—the CEO who had requested the training, their own manager, who would need to approve the budget, and the customer service manager. But e-mail use affected everyone in the organization, so they felt it would be important to gain the support of all the managers by soliciting their ideas and keeping them informed.
- The audience for training was potentially large, with very diverse needs, and scattered in branch offices throughout the country. Boris and Marietta decided to recommend starting out with training in the home office for people who had direct e-mail contact with customers. Once that program was launched, they could look at adapting it for other groups.
- They identified several people who needed to be involved in the training program design process, including their manager, someone from IT, someone from legal, the customer service manager, and at least two subject-matter experts, one for the legal implications of e-mail and one for written communication skills, and representatives of the target audience.

Quick Quiz

List the three to five key learning points from this chapter that will be most helpful to you.

____

____

____

____

____

What's Next?

Determining that there is a real need for training and clarifying the desired outcome gives you a great start. The next step is to develop the learning objectives that specify what people will be able to do as a result of training and form the foundation for measuring the program's success. That's what you'll learn to do in the next chapter.

Apply What You Learn

Use the questions below to analyze your training project:

1. How will you gather information? What method(s) will you use?

   ____

   ____

   ____

   ____

2. What change is needed? What is the gap between the current situation and the desired outcome?

   ____

   ____

   ____

   ____

   How urgent or important is it to change the current situation? What if nothing is done?

   ____

   ____

What are the reasons for the performance gap?

____

____

Is training the best way to achieve the desired outcome? One of the ways?

____

____

3. Who are the stakeholders? Which stakeholders have decision-making authority? What will you do to involve stakeholders early in the process?

____

____

____

____

____

____

4. What are the characteristics of the learners? What jobs do they do?

____

____

How large is the audience?

____

Where are learners located?

____

What kind of time do learners have available for training?

____

(*Continued*)

Are learners self-selecting or is this training mandated?

____

What do they know about why this training is being held?

____

____

In terms of this topic, what do they already know/are they able to do?

____

____

____

____

____

____

What do they need to know or be able to do as a result of training?

____

____

____

____

____

____

What previous experiences have they had with training? How do they prefer to learn?

____

____

____

____

Are they from the same or different areas of the organization? The same or different levels? Do they know one another?

Will managers and their direct reports be taking the same training at the same time? ☐ Yes ☐ No ☐ Maybe

5. What are the constraints and other factors that impact the training design? Can this training program be purchased or adapted from an existing program? Does it need to be designed from scratch?

6. Who needs to be involved in the process of designing the training program? Management? Trainees? Instructional designers and materials developers? Other HR professionals? Subject-matter experts?

Answers to Exercises

Check What You Know

Which statements about gathering information are accurate?

1. ____ When interviewing people, it's a good idea to use leading questions to keep the discussion on the right track.
2. ____ Surveys and questionnaires provide the most useful information because they are the most objective.
3. _ X _ Although tests help you learn what people do and do not know, they do not usually provide much information about why a performance gap exists.
4. _ X _ The value of collecting information by observation is that you can compare what people really do to what they or others say they do.
5. ____ The key to a useful survey is including as many relevant questions as you can.

Quick Quiz

If you were interviewing a manager to gather information about how well the team leaders in his department run meetings, which of the following would be useful questions?

1. ____ Are you happy with the way your team leaders run meetings?

2. _X_ What, if anything, would you like team leaders to change about the way they run meetings? Why?
3. _X_ Could you please describe the way that your team leaders run meetings?
4. ____ Do you have any team leaders who don't have a clue about how to run a meeting? Who are they?
5. ____ Do your team leaders need training on running meetings?

THINK ABOUT IT

In which of the following situations is change "nice-to-have"? In which is change important but not urgent? In which is change important and urgent?

N = Nice to have
I = Important but not urgent
UI = Urgent and important

1. __UI__ Significant changes in governmental regulations that affect the way in which loan applications are processed will take place in three months.
2. __N__ Sales assistants have expressed interest in learning how to use PowerPoint to make presentations so that they can take on new responsibilities.
3. __UI__ During the past six months, an increasing number of top performers have left the company for competing organizations, and their exit interviews indicated that nearly 25 per cent were unhappy with their relationships with their managers.
4. __I__ Customers have been complaining that they have to wait on the phone for long periods before they can reach a support person with a problem or question.

Check What You Know

For each of the situations below, list some possible reasons for the performance gap and think about some of the ways, other than training, to effect change in these situations:

Your answers may differ.

1. Company policy is that all the managers do a formal performance appraisal for each of their employees at least once a year. Nearly 35 percent of the managers are doing the appraisals late, doing them incorrectly, or not doing them at all.

   Possible reasons: The corporate culture places little value on the performance appraisal process; the performance appraisal procedures are cumbersome, confusing, and unclear; managers do not think they have enough time.

   Ways other than training to effect change: Have executives and senior managers demonstrate the importance of regular appraisals by doing them for their direct reports; revise the procedures so appraisals are easier to do correctly; evaluate managers' workloads to make sure that they have the time needed to conduct appraisals.

2. A hospital that serves a large population without health insurance has emergency room wait times of up to twelve hours. The new director wants to cut the maximum wait time in half by the end of the year.

   Possible reasons: Understaffing; lack of examining rooms or cubicles; confusing or unclear admittance and screening procedures.

   Ways other than training to effect change: Hire more staff and find more space; revise admittance and screening procedures so they are clearer and easier to follow.

3. A nonprofit legal clinic offers free or low-cost advice to people whose income falls below a certain level. To use the attorneys' time most efficiently, the clinic uses volunteers who screen clients to make sure they qualify for services and gather information about their need for legal services by asking a series of questions. The clinic manager has noticed that the volunteers, who sign up for three-hour shifts once a week, often sit around with nothing to do.

   Possible reasons: The staff is signing up too many volunteers for each shift; no one is responsible for coordinating client appointments with volunteer availability.

   Ways other than training to effect change: Sign up fewer volunteers for each shift; give one staff member the responsibility of coordinating client appointments with volunteer availability.

3
Writing Learning Objectives

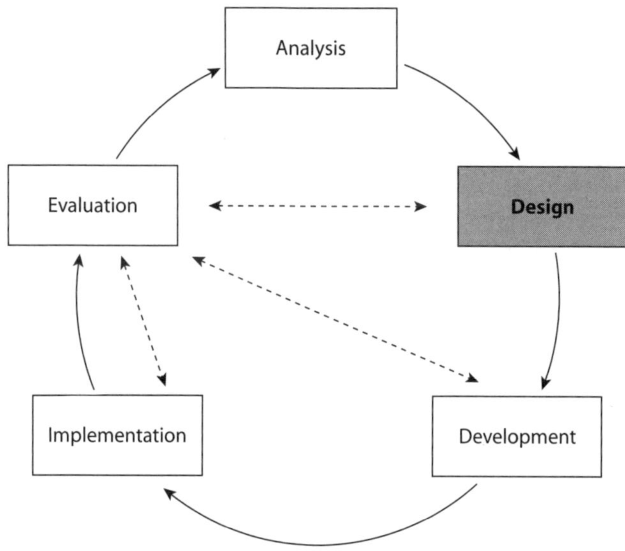

Design Stage of the ADDIE Model

Check What You Know

Boris and Marietta's manager agreed with their conclusions about the best ways to help employees improve their use of e-mail. "I'll see what I can do about distributing the written policies to everyone in the organization," he said. "While I'm working on that, you can start planning the training program."

Boris and Marietta knew that their next task would be to write the learning objectives for the program—statements that would express exactly what learners will be able to do when the program is completed. Can you think of what some of those objectives might be?

____

____

____

____

My son started playing soccer at the age of six. The kids were very cute and fun to watch, but most of them didn't really know where the goal was or even what the goal looked like—one adorable little boy used to stand in the middle of the field playing with the zipper on his jacket while the ball flew by him. If these pint-sized soccer players hadn't learned how to recognize the goal by the time they started playing real games, they would have been at a clear disadvantage—they'd have been able to score only by accident. It's the same with training. To design a program that helps learners achieve the desired outcome, you need to have a very clear idea of where you are going and know what the goal looks like. In this chapter, you'll learn to write learning objectives that will serve as the basis both for developing your training program and for evaluating its success.

What's in this chapter:

- Why learning objectives matter
- What a learning objective looks like

- What makes a learning objective useful
- How to develop learning objectives and enabling objectives

An objective is a description of a performance you want learners to be able to exhibit before you consider them competent. An objective describes an intended result of instruction, rather than the process of instruction itself.

Robert F. Mager,
Preparing Instructional Objectives

1. Why Learning Objectives Matter

Check What You Know

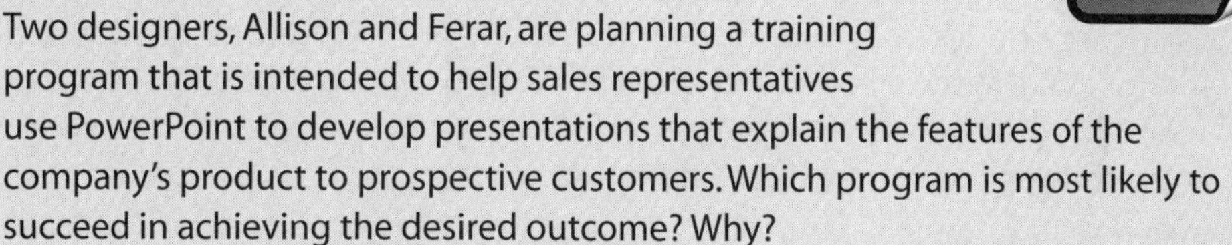

Two designers, Allison and Ferar, are planning a training program that is intended to help sales representatives use PowerPoint to develop presentations that explain the features of the company's product to prospective customers. Which program is most likely to succeed in achieving the desired outcome? Why?

1. ____ Allison lists all of PowerPoint's features and describes the various ways in which PowerPoint can be used. She then develops a detailed outline that shows the sequence in which those topics will be taught.
2. ____ Ferer lists everything that the sales associates need to be able to do in order to use PowerPoint to develop sales presentations that illustrate the product's features. He then develops written statements that express exactly what learners will be able to do as a result of training and uses those statements to identify the topics to cover.

You probably realized that Ferar's approach, which focuses on what learners need to be able to do, instead of what they need to know, is more likely to succeed. Ferar is identifying the learning objectives—what people need to be able to do by the time they finish training. He understands that it's not the process of learning about all of PowerPoint's features that's important; the topics his program covers will be determined by the needs of the job—what knowledge and skills people actually need so they can prepare sales presentations.

Alison, on the other hand, never stopped to consider what was important in terms of the desired outcome of training. As a result, the people in her program may waste time learning about features they will never use, and they still might leave the program without being able to prepare presentations that help to sell the company's product.

Learning objectives are written descriptions of the goal—the situation that will exist when training has been completed. In other words, before training, the sales reps are unable to use PowerPoint to prepare presentations; after training—*as a result of training*—they will be able to do so.

Learning objectives serve several important purposes:

- *Objectives tell you where you are going so you can figure out the best way (content, activities, methodology, media, materials) to get there*. In that way, objectives are similar to an itinerary for a trip. Suppose you are traveling from San Francisco to a family reunion in Savannah, Georgia, and you'd like to make three stops along the way. Your first step will be to figure out what those stops will be. Then you can figure out the best way to reach each of them as you head for Savannah.
- *Objectives help you focus on what's important*. As you'll see, the learn-ing objectives provide the basis for key decisions about such things as the delivery method, the content, and the activities. The objectives can also determine how long the program will be, if that decision has not already been made. Perhaps most importantly, the objectives help you sort through the available content so you can decide what to include—not too much, not too little, but (to paraphrase Goldilocks), just the right amount!
- *Objectives provide the basis for measuring the success of the training*. If your destination is Yellowstone Park, and you know what signposts to look for (such as a gushing geyser), you will know when you have arrived. In fact, well-written learning objectives provide those signposts, making it possible to evaluate how well the program has done what it set out to do.

- *Objectives provide a clear purpose and destination for the learners.* Adult learners do better when they know what they are going to learn and why it's important. Just as the learning objectives help to focus you on what's important as you design and develop the training program, the objectives help learners understand where they are going and see how the program's content and activities will help them get there.

> *Research on learning demonstrates the value of clarifying to the learners what it is they will be able to do by the end of the lesson, module, or course . . . . If the learners know what they are supposed to learn, research suggests that there's a better chance that they will learn it.*
>
> Harold D. Stolovitch and Erica J. Keeps, *Telling Ain't Training*

2. What a Learning Objective Should Be

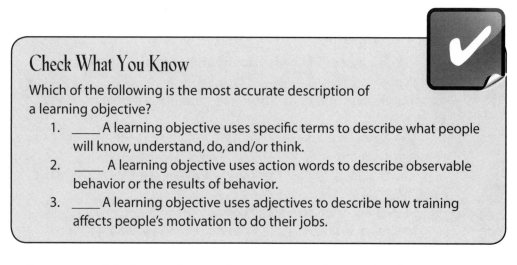

Check What You Know

Which of the following is the most accurate description of a learning objective?

1. ____ A learning objective uses specific terms to describe what people will know, understand, do, and/or think.
2. ____ A learning objective uses action words to describe observable behavior or the results of behavior.
3. ____ A learning objective uses adjectives to describe how training affects people's motivation to do their jobs.

Instructional designers do not always agree on how to conduct a needs assessment or what training methods are most effective. But although they may use different terminology, the people who design and develop training programs generally agree on what constitutes a useful learning objective.

In its essential form, a learning objective is a written statement that describes the outcome of training. A learning objective . . .

- Describes what the learner will be able *to do* when training is completed
- Is expressed in behavioral, measurable terms
- Uses action words (write, explain, identify, repair, and so on)
- Always describes performance (what learner will be able to do)
- May also describe the conditions (the circumstances under which learners will be able to perform) and standards (the criteria the performance will meet: how many, how fast, how well)

Quick Quiz

Which of the following statements meet the criteria described above for a learning objective?

1. ____ Given a description of a customer and a situation, demonstrate how to open a sales call.
2. ____ Understand how to use the seven steps in the problem-solving process.
3. ____ Create an Excel spreadsheet that compares expenditures for two consecutive quarters.
4. ____ Given a simulated feedback session with an employee, use active listening.
5. ____ Know how to create a project plan.
6. ____ Identify questions that are inappropriate to ask during a hiring interview.

The key question to ask when developing a learning objective is, "How will you know that the learner has achieved this objective?" How will you know, for example, that someone understands or appreciates something? Learned something? Knows something? Feels something? You can only know those things through people's actions or the results of their actions.

Components of a Learning Objective

According to Robert F. Mager, the expert on training and human performance improvement issues who is widely known for having introduced behavioral objectives to educators and trainers in the early 1960s, behavioral learning objectives generally include three components:

- *The objective.* A description of performance or behavior that includes an action word (a verb): *Change* a tire; *prepare* a work plan; *answer* customers' questions. Every learning objective must include this description. The description must clearly state what learners will *do* to demonstrate that they have achieved the objective, not what they will know, or learn, or understand, or feel. Even if training is intended to help people understand something or change their attitudes toward something, the learning objective must describe something that can be observed—either behavior or the results of behavior.
- *The conditions.* Many, although not all, learning objectives include a description of the conditions under which the learner will be expected to perform: *Given tools, a truck with a flat tire, and a job aid*, change the tire; *given a project description and a checklist*, prepare a work plan; *given a customer service manual*, answer customers' questions. The conditions narrow the objective by specifying the circumstances. It's like saying, "I'll arrive in

Clarifying the Conditions

Here are examples of conditions under which learners will be expected to demonstrate that they have mastered a learning objective:

- Given access to a search engine ...
- Without reference ...
- Given a case study ...
- Using a simulation ...
- After viewing a video clip ...
- With the help of a job aid ...

Savannah at 6 p.m. on October 7, *as long as my flight is not delayed or my car doesn't break down on the way to the airport.*" Not all learning objectives include conditions. Sometimes there aren't any, and sometimes they can be assumed. But for clarity, it's best to include anything learners must have or any situational factors that affect whether or how well learners can achieve the objective.

> *Having described what you want students to be able to do, you can increase the communication power of an objective by telling them HOW WELL you want them to be able to do it. . . . A criterion is the standard by which performance is evaluated, the yardstick by which achievement of the objective is assessed.*
>
> Robert F. Mager,
> *Preparing Instructional Objectives*

Clarifying the Standards

Robert Mager describes three ways to specify the standard or criterion in a learning objective: speed, accuracy, and quality.

- *Speed.* How quickly does the learner need to perform—Within ten minutes? Thirty minutes? Two hours?

  Example: Using a job aid and a tool kit, assemble a mountain bicycle within forty-five minutes.

- *Accuracy.* How well does the learner need to perform—Without error? With fewer than five mistakes?

  Example: Given a video clip with a simulated job interview, identify all the illegal questions the interviewer asks.

- *Quality.* Does the performance meet a specific standard of quality?

  Example: Given necessary information and sample reports, prepare an annual report that meets the standards on a checklist.

- *Standard (criterion)*. Most objectives include a description of the standard or standards for performance that the learner will be expected to meet: How many? How soon? How fast? How well? Change the tire *within five minutes so that it meets the criteria in the technical manual*; prepare a work plan that *specifies the actions, responsibilities, expected outcomes, and deadlines as shown on the checklist*; answer customer's questions correctly *at least 95 percent of the time*.

  The standard provides additional clarification. Not only will I arrive in Savannah, but I will arrive *by 6 P.M. on October 7*. That deadline offers a way to measure how successful I will be at achieving the objective. Like conditions, not all learning objectives include standards. But also like conditions, standards add clarity to an objective and provide specifics that help you evaluate the learner's performance.

From the Learner's Point of View

In his book, *Designing and Assessing Courses and Curricula*, Robert M. Diamond suggests another way to think about learning objectives: Imagine the learners asking what they need to do at the end of the training program to convince you that they have learned what they were supposed to learn."Out of this discussion," writes Dr. Diamond,"will come performance objectives that are measurable and that tend to be far more important.... than would be produced otherwise."

- *Quality*. According to Mager, "Many times the speed and/or accuracy of a performance are not the critical criteria. Instead, something about the quality of the performance must be present if the performance is to be considered acceptable."

  Sometimes it's relatively easy to describe the acceptable quality: the performance or the result of performance meets all the criteria on a checklist, or a panel of experts judges it acceptable. But it can take careful thinking to identify a standard of quality that can be measured. You might need several tries to answer the question, "How will I know whether the learner has successfully achieved this objective?"

THINK ABOUT IT

What are some observable actions, or the results of actions, that demonstrate that a learner …

1. Understands the seven steps in the problem-solving process?

2. Knows how to balance a checkbook?

3. Is willing to accept constructive criticism?

4. Appreciates the importance of meeting deadlines?

5. Knows how to follow safety procedures?

____

____

____

____

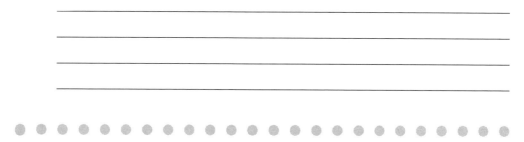

3. What Makes a Learning Objective Useful?

There are learning objectives, and then there are learning objectives: some are more useful than others. Learning objectives that provide a solid basis for decisions about the program content and the training methods are those that meet the following criteria:

- They are clearly related to the desired outcome of training.
- They are relevant and meaningful.
- They describe something that learners can reasonably be expected to do.

Clearly Related to the Desired Outcome of Training

Using specific, unambiguous language, well-written, useful learning objectives answer the question, "What do people need to know or be able to do to achieve this outcome?"

THINK ABOUT IT

You are designing a training program that is intended to help high school seniors apply for summer jobs. What are some of the things that the teenagers might need to know or be able to do to achieve the desired outcome?

____

____

____

____

One of the things that the teenagers would need to know is how to fill out a job application. Another would be how to prepare for a job interview. Thus, when the training has been completed, the teenagers would *be able to fill out a job application* and *prepare for a job interview*. If by the end of the training program, the teenagers could accomplish those learning objectives and the others that you identified, the program would have achieved its desired results.

Relevant and Meaningful

A learning objective should describe something that people need to be able to do to achieve a goal *and* that is worth doing.

Quick Quiz

For the training program to teach teenagers to apply for a summer job, which of the following objectives describes both what they need to be able to do and something that is worth doing:

1. ___ Find three postings that describe jobs that meet your requirements and for which you are qualified.
2. ___ List three sources of information about summer jobs.

The first objective above describes something that the teenagers need to be able to do when they begin their job search. Being able to list sources of information will help them find job postings, but it doesn't describe performance that is useful on its own. It is what instructional designers call an "enabling" objective, one that helps learners achieve a learning objective. (There's more on enabling objectives later in this chapter.)

Describe Something That Learners Can Reasonably Be Expected to Do

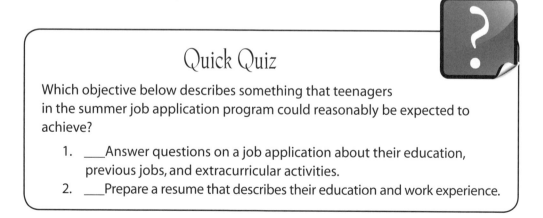

Quick Quiz

Which objective below describes something that teenagers in the summer job application program could reasonably be expected to achieve?

1. ___Answer questions on a job application about their education, previous jobs, and extracurricular activities.
2. ___Prepare a resume that describes their education and work experience.

People who apply for professional jobs need to be able to prepare a resume. But although it would be nice for a teenager to have such a skill, it would be unreasonable to expect a resume from a teenager applying for a summer job. Not only would their prospective employers be unlikely to require resumes, but few teenagers have amassed enough work experience for a resume.

S.M.A.R.T. Objectives

One way to make sure that learning objectives are as useful as possible is to follow the SMART guidelines.

Check What You Know

When it comes to training, what do you think the letters in the SMART acronym stand for?

S ______________________________

M ______________________________

A ______________________________

R ______________________________

T ______________________________

Here's what the letters typically stand for:

Specific. A SMART objective uses specific language, including action words that describe what learners will be able to do as a result of training. *Example: Fill out* a job application.

Measurable. A SMART objective describes actions that can be observed or measured in some way. *Example:* Fill out a job application *accurately and completely according to the criteria on a checklist.*

Achievable. A SMART objective is realistic. It describes something that people will actually be able to do, given the right situation, tools, equipment, and so on. It also describes something that can be attained by the end of the training program. *Example: Given a blank job application and the criteria on a checklist,* fill out the job application accurately and completely.

Relevant. A SMART objective is meaningful and clearly related to the desired outcome of the program. *Example: To be able to apply for a job,* teenagers need to know how to fill out a job application.

Timely. A SMART objective is important now. *Example:* Teenagers will be applying for jobs *as soon as they complete the training program.*

4. How to Develop Learning Objectives

Writing the learning objectives is the first step in the Design stage of the ADDIE process. In reality, you might already have a pretty good idea of what the learning objectives are by the time you reach that stage. In fact, many instructional design projects begin with preliminary objectives.

Before you can write the learning objectives that you will use to make the other crucial design decisions, however, you need to know the following:

- *What the training program is intended to accomplish.* It stands to reason that you can't write learning objectives to achieve a desired outcome until you know what that outcome is.
- *The learners' starting place vis-à-vis the subject.* If the goal is to teach sales representatives to use PowerPoint to prepare a presentation, what do they already know about PowerPoint? Do they know what it is? Can they already use its basic features? Do they have any preconceptions about PowerPoint that might need to change?
- *What is being taught.* Learning to change a tire is different from learning the bones in the human body or learning to work with a group to achieve consensus. It's easier to come up with the right learning objectives when you have a good understanding of what is being taught (you'll learn more about the types of learning below).

Types of Learning

When writing objectives, it helps to understand that there are different types of learning. The three broad categories, often called "domains," which were identified in the 1950s by Dr. Benjamin Bloom and a group of colleagues at the University of Chicago, are "Knowledge," "Skills," and "Attitude," often referred to as "KSAs." The verbs that describe what learners will know or be able to do as a result of training are somewhat different for each category. (The instructional methods for each type of learning also differ, as you will learn later in this book.)

- *Knowledge*. Also known as the cognitive domain, this category refers to intellectual activity, such as acquiring information, analyzing and evaluating, and applying knowledge. Examples of action verbs in the objectives for this type of learning include define, describe, select, name, discuss, explain, use, identify, compare, justify, and distinguish. For example, learners will be able to . . .

  Describe the government regulations that auditors must comply with

  Write a proposal for funding in response to a Request for Proposal from a foundation

  Use the interviewing guidelines to interview a candidate for a position

  Identify ways to improve customer service procedures

  Explain the reasons for providing an agenda for meetings

  Discuss the factors that affect hiring decisions

- *Skills*. Also known as the psychomotor domain, this category refers to manual or physical skills that require practice to attain. Action verbs in the objectives for this type of learning include assemble, organize, measure, respond, design, create, and repair. For example, learners will be able to . . .

  Replace the brake pads on a delivery truck

  Design the layout for a training workshop

  Assemble the components of a home theater system

  Create posters for a marketing campaign

- *Attitude*. Also known as the affective domain, this category refers to feelings, emotions, and values. Action verbs for the objectives include demonstrate, choose, discuss, respond, listen, and participate. For example, learners will be able to . . .

  Listen while other people are talking.

  Participate actively in discussions.

Smile when greeting customers.

Respect other people's points of view even when you disagree.

Wear appropriate business clothing as described in the employee manual.

Objectives for Learning That Involves Attitudes

When the intent of training is to bring about a change in learners' skills or knowledge, it's relatively easy to come up with action verbs that describe what they will be able to do as a result of training. But identifying the learning objectives can be difficult when the purpose of training is to bring about a change in people's attitudes.

Suppose a goal of the training program is to change the way that people interact with customers. You want them to be more considerate of customers, but you can't observe or measure whether someone is willing to do that or how he or she feels about doing it. What you can do is observe people's behavior or the results of their behavior in real or simulated situations. For example, you can see whether someone smiles at customers and greets them by name, listens when they voice concerns, takes the time to answer their questions, and so on. You could also ask customers questions about how they were treated.

To write the learning objectives, ask yourself: What behavior (smiling, calling people by their names) or results of behavior (positive responses from customers) would indicate that a learner's attitude had changed?

Writing Learning Objectives

Below is a process you can follow to write the learning objectives for your training program. You will draw on all the information that you collected during the analysis, including any preliminary objectives that may already have been identified. As you work, you might find that you need to stop and gather more information before you can proceed.

1. Review all the information you have. Then write down everything that learners might need to know or be able to do to achieve the desired outcome of the program.

   Example: For managers to conduct hiring interviews, they need to be able to . . .

   - Schedule a hiring interview
   - Know which prospects are qualified
   - Know what questions to ask job candidates
   - Learn which questions they cannot legally ask
   - Understand how to ask questions that elicit useful information
   - Know what information to give candidates
   - [etc.]

2. Cross off the list anything that participants already know or are able to do, or that is not necessary for them to achieve the desired outcome. For example, if managers' responsibilities do not include screening resumes or scheduling interviews, or if they already know how to do those things, objectives for those topics would not be necessary.

3. Turn the remaining items on the list into learning objectives that meet the criteria, with conditions and/or standards as needed.

How Many Learning Objectives?

There are no hard-and-fast rules about how many learning objectives to address in a given training program. But there are practical considerations. The learning objectives determine how much content and how many activities to include in the program, so the more objectives, the longer the program will be. The amount of time learners will have available for training, as well as the amount of time and other resources you have to develop the program, establish natural limits on the number of objectives that can be achieved—and thus, on the program outcome.

Example: During a simulated job interview:

Given a job description and a resume, ask questions that elicit information about a candidate's qualifications for the job, according to a checklist, and that comply with legal guidelines.

4. Check each objective against the SMART criteria.

5. Enabling Objectives

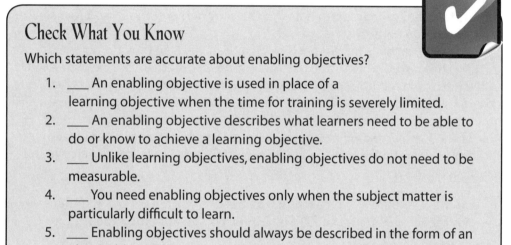

Check What You Know

Which statements are accurate about enabling objectives?

1. ___ An enabling objective is used in place of a learning objective when the time for training is severely limited.
2. ___ An enabling objective describes what learners need to be able to do or know to achieve a learning objective.
3. ___ Unlike learning objectives, enabling objectives do not need to be measurable.
4. ___ You need enabling objectives only when the subject matter is particularly difficult to learn.
5. ___ Enabling objectives should always be described in the form of an observable action.

For any trip, there are the primary destinations and lots of little destinations along the way. To reach Seattle from Houston, you need to go from your home to the airport, through the security line to the gate, from the gate to the plane . . . you get the idea. For training programs, the primary destinations are called *terminal* objectives, and the little destinations along the way are *enabling* objectives. (Instructional designers may use different terminology, but the idea remains the same.)

An enabling objective describes what learners need to be able to do and/or know to achieve a learning objective. For novice mechanics to be able to change a truck tire, they first have to be able to recognize and use the tools they will need. For team leaders to be able to prepare a work plan, they first need to know what a work plan is and how it is used. For customer service representatives to be able to answer customers' questions, they need to know where to look up the answers and what to do if they are unable to find an answer.

Just as the learning objectives come from the question, "What do learners need to know or be able to do to achieve the desired outcome?" enabling objectives come from the question, "What do learners need to know or be able to do to achieve this learning objective?" As you will learn in later chapters, the enabling objectives help you select the content, activities, and structure to help learners achieve each of the learning objectives. The process of identifying the enabling objectives for each learning objective leads directly to a working outline that makes it easier to develop the program and keeps you focused on the desired outcome.

Enabling objectives do not need to be measurable, so they do not need to include standards or conditions. Although they should always be expressed in the form of an action, the action verbs do not always need to describe observable behavior or results of behavior—"know," "understand,""learn," and "consider" can be perfectly good verbs to use when writing enabling objectives. Here are some examples. You can see that the enabling objectives indicate content that will be needed for participants to be able to achieve the learning objective.

Learning Objective: Given a list of prospective customers and their telephone numbers, make cold calls to obtain in-person appointments.

Enabling Objectives:

Understand the purpose of a cold call

Learn what to say when making cold calls

Know how to interpret the codes on a customer list

Learning Objective: Given an opening procedures checklist, prepare the store to open for business by 10:00 A.M.

Enabling Objectives:

Understand the security procedures

Learn how to set up the checkout station

Know how to get help with problems

Quick Quiz

Suppose you were designing a training program to help people buy a car. One of the learning objectives is below. What are some of the enabling objectives—what would people need to know or be able to do to achieve that learning objective?

Learning objective: Given a description of a car that includes make, model, and features, find the best price within a fifty-mile radius of your home.

Enabling objective:

___

Enabling objective:

___

Enabling objective:

___

Boris and Marietta's Progress

Boris and Marietta have identified the following learning objectives for the e-mail program.

When participants complete this training program, they will be able to:

- Given the company's written e-mail policies and examples of e-mail messages to customers, identify the messages that contain inappropriate information with 100 percent accuracy.

(*Continued*)

- Given necessary information, write an e-mail message that is sent to the right readers, conveys the main points clearly, includes the right information, is organized so the message is easy to follow, uses the right tone, and has a useful subject line, as rated "good" or better on a checklist.
- Given an e-mail message with errors in the use of language, grammar, and punctuation, identify and correct the errors with 90 percent accuracy.
- Develop an action plan for improving their use of e-mail time that includes specific action steps they will take during the next three months.

Boris and Marietta also identified the enabling objectives for each of the learning objectives. Some of their enabling objectives are shown below. Notice how the enabling objectives point to the content for that part of the training program.

Learning Objective: Given the company's written e-mail policies and examples of e-mail messages to customers, identify the messages that contain inappropriate information with 100 percent accuracy.

- Recognize content that is not appropriate in an e-mail message to customers.
- Understand the potential consequences of including inappropriate content in an e-mail message.

Learning Objective: Given necessary information, write an e-mail message that is sent to the right readers, conveys the main points clearly, includes the right information, is organized so the message is easy to follow, uses the right tone, and has a useful subject line, as rated "good" or better on a checklist,

- Determine who should and should not receive an e-mail message,
- Know how and when to use distribution lists.
- Understand the importance of looking at what they are writing from their reader's point of view.

- Understand the difference between writing to influence and writing to inform.
- Formulate a statement that expresses their most important message.
- Learn how to use a step-by-step process to decide what information to include in an e-mail message.
- Organize information so that readers can easily follow points,
- Know when and how to use headings and lists.
- Understand the factors that influence tone.
- Learn the criteria for a useful subject line.

Quick Quiz

List the three to five key learning points from this chapter that will be most helpful to you.

____

____

____

____

____

What's Next?

You know how to get started on your training program design by writing the learning objectives that express what participants will accomplish. In the next chapter, you'll learn how to make a very important decision: What delivery method or methods would be best for the learners and the situation?

Apply What You Learn

Use the worksheet on page 97 to write learning objectives for your training program and enabling objectives for one learning objective.

Answers to Exercises

Check What You Know

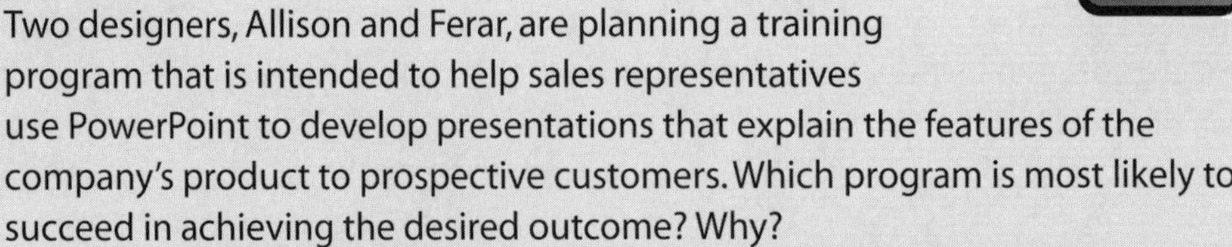

Two designers, Allison and Ferar, are planning a training program that is intended to help sales representatives use PowerPoint to develop presentations that explain the features of the company's product to prospective customers. Which program is most likely to succeed in achieving the desired outcome? Why?

1. ___ Allison lists all of PowerPoint's features and describes the various ways in which PowerPoint can be used. She then develops a detailed outline that shows the sequence in which those topics will be taught.
2. _X_ Ferer lists everything that the sales associates need to be able to do in order to use PowerPoint to develop sales presentations that illustrate the product's features. He then develops written statements that express exactly what learners will be able to do as a result of training and uses those statements to identify the topics to cover.

   In Ferar's program, the topics will be determined by the knowledge and skills people actually need so they can prepare sales presentations. In Allison's program, people might learn about features they will never use, yet still leave without being able to prepare the sales presentations.

Check What You Know

Which of the following is the most accurate description of a learning objective?

1. ___ A learning objective uses specific terms to describe what people will know, understand, do, and/or think.
2. _X_ A learning objective uses action words to describe observable behavior or the results of behavior.
3. ___ A learning objective uses adjectives to describe how training affects people's motivation to do their jobs.

Quick Quiz

Which of the following statements meet the criteria described above for a learning objective?

1. _X_ Given a description of a customer and a situation, demonstrate how to open a sales call.
2. ___ Understand how to use the seven steps in the problem-solving process.
3. _X_ Create an Excel spreadsheet that compares expenditures for two consecutive quarters.
4. _X_ Given a simulated feedback session with an employee, use active listening.
5. ___ Know how to create a project plan.
6. _X_ Identify questions that are inappropriate to ask during a hiring interview.

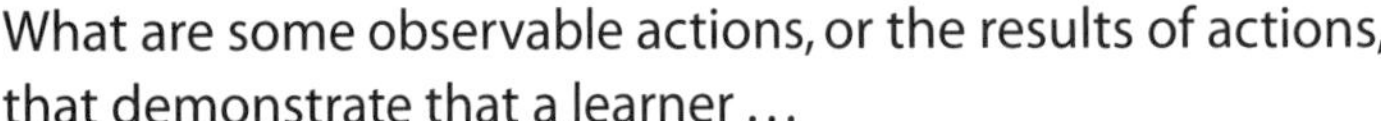

THINK ABOUT IT

What are some observable actions, or the results of actions, that demonstrate that a learner . . .

You might have come up with observable actions or results that are similar to these:

1. Understands the seven steps in the problem-solving process?
   - *Describes the seven steps in the problem-solving process*
   - *Uses the seven steps in the problem-solving process to come up with a solution for a given problem*
2. Knows how to balance a checkbook?
   - *Balances a checkbook*
   - *Explains the process for balancing a checkbook*
3. Is willing to accept constructive criticism?
   - *Listens to constructive criticism without arguing*
   - *Demonstrates a willingness to accept constructive criticism by listening to criticism delivered by a supervisor*
4. Appreciates the importance of meeting deadlines?
   - *Meets all deadlines*
   - *Explains the reasons why it is important to meet deadlines*
5. *Knows how to follow* safety procedures?
   - *Follows all posted safety procedures*
   - *Describes what needs to done to follow safety procedures*

Quick Quiz

For the program to teach teenagers to apply for a summer job, which of the following objectives describes both what they need to be able to do and something that is worth doing:

1. _X_ Find three postings that describe jobs that meet your requirements and for which you are qualified.
2. ___ List three sources of information about summer jobs.

Quick Quiz

Which objective below describes something that teenagers in the summer job application program could reasonably be expected to achieve?

1. _X_ Answer questions on a job application about their education, previous jobs, and extracurricular activities.
2. ___ Prepare a resume that describes their education and work experience.

Check What You Know

Which statements are accurate about enabling objectives?

1. ___ An enabling objective is used in place of a learning objective when the time for training is severely limited.
2. _X_ An enabling objective describes what learners need to be able to do or know to achieve a learning objective.
3. _X_ Unlike learning objectives, enabling objectives do not need to be measurable.
4. ___ You need enabling objectives only when the subject matter is particularly difficult to learn.
5. _X_ Enabling objectives should always be described in the form of an observable action.

Quick Quiz

Suppose you were designing a training program to help people buy a car. One of the learning objectives is below. What are some of the enabling objectives—what would people need to know or be able to do to achieve that learning objective?

The enabling objectives you came up with might be similar to the ones shown below:

Learning objective: Given a description of a car that includes make, model, and features, find the best price within a fifty-mile radius of your home.

Enabling objective: Know what questions to ask when contacting dealers

Enabling objective: Understand the way that dealers price vehicles

Enabling objective: Determine whether it is better to call, e-mail, or visit a dealer to get information

Worksheet

Writing Objectives

Title or brief description of training program: ______________________

____

Brief description of desired outcome: ______________________

____

What learners need to know or be able to do when the program is completed:

____

____

____

____

____

____

Learning objectives (each with an action verb that describes observable behavior or the results of behavior; the conditions, if any; and the standard for measurement—how many, how fast, how well)

Objective 1:

____

____

Conditions:

____

____

Standard:

____

____

(*Continued*)

Objective 2:

Conditions:

Standard:

Objective 3:

Conditions:

Standard:

Objective 4:

Conditions:

Standard:

Objective 5:

___

___

Conditions:

___

___

Standard:

___

___

Enabling Objectives for Learning Objective 1

___

___

___

___

___

___

___

___

4

Choosing the Delivery Method

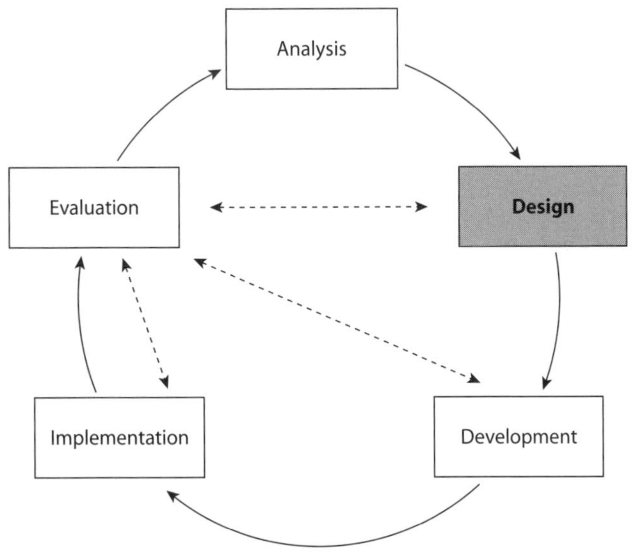

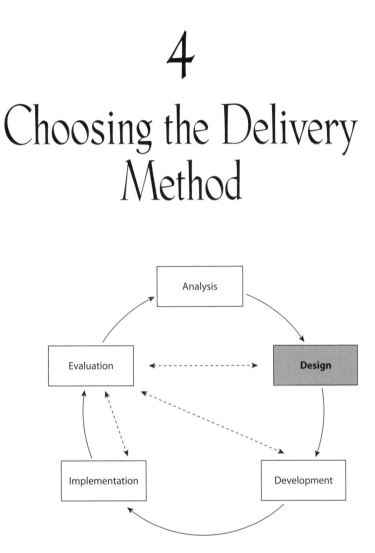

The Design Stage of the ADDIE Model

Check What You Know

Now that Boris and Marietta have developed the learning objectives for the e-mail program, their next task is to determine the best way to deliver the training.

"I thought we were supposed to develop a workshop," Marietta said. "Isn't that what the CEO asked for?"

"She did," Boris said. "At least a workshop is what she mentioned. But there are other ways to deliver training. Before we start putting together a workshop, we should at least consider whether that's the best way, or the only way, to help people improve their use of e-mail."

Boris and Marietta are smart not to assume that a workshop is the best way to deliver the e-mail training. What other methods might work as well, or better? What factors should they consider when making this important decision?

____

____

____

____

____

____

When you ship a package, you have lots of options: the postal service, express delivery services, courier services, ground shipping services, and more. Your choice is determined by a variety of factors, including where the package is going, how quickly it needs to arrive, its size, the value of the contents, and the costs of the different options. You have the same kinds of choices when you travel—the transportation method you choose depends on how far you need to go, whether there is an ocean between you and your destination, how quickly you need to be there, whether you need to work en route, which modes of transportation you prefer—and, of course, the cost.

To decide on the best way to deliver training, you'll consider some of the same factors—destination (the program goals), urgency (how quickly training has to be delivered), size (the number of people to be trained), preferences (of learners and stakeholders), content (what needs to be learned), available resources (including expertise) and the cost of different delivery methods.

What you'll learn in this chapter will help you consider those factors so you can make the right decision.

What's in this chapter:

- Overview of the ways in which training is delivered
- Characteristics of the types of delivery methods
- How to choose the right delivery method

> *. . . live or virtual, synchronous or asynchronous, on-the-job or in the classroom, one-on-one or one-on-many or many-on-one, face-to-face or technology delivered. . . . it's all the same in terms of learning.*
>
> Harold D. Stolovitch and Erica J. Keeps, *Telling Ain't Training*

1. Overview of Training Delivery Methods

Unless you've been living in a cave without a cell phone or Internet access, you know that there have been enormous changes in the workplace during the past few decades. Most of those changes can be directly linked to the increasing use of technology. Many team members now work in widely separated locations. Telecommuting is on the rise. The Internet and technological tools have made it possible for people to communicate easily across vast distances and different time zones. When I was a child, the video phone was the stuff of science fiction; recently, *The New York Times* ran an article on grandparents who regularly use videocams to "visit" their grandchildren.

Technology has also brought training into the new century, making it possible—and, because of workplace changes, often necessary—to deliver training in new ways. Still, some things have stayed much the same: although various forms of e-learning—training delivered via computer—are increasing rapidly, ASTD's 2007 State of the Industry Report tells us that more than 65 percent of training is still delivered through live instructor-led workshops and seminars. That's not surprising. The classroom is a familiar place—we've all spent a lot of time there. Workshops can be put together relatively easily and inexpensively when compared to the complexity and cost of a highly customized e-learning program. And let's face it—the most sophisticated technology will never be able to match the value of getting people together in the same place, where they can explore concepts, share ideas, and learn from one another.

But even though people often assume that "training" means "workshop," many situations call for other delivery methods. Just as you'd want to know all your options for shipping a package or traveling to a specific destination, you need to understand all the options for delivering training so that you can choose the methods that are most likely to achieve the desired outcome and provide the organization with a reasonable return on its investment.

Two Types of Delivery Methods

Check What You Know

Training methods fall into two primary categories: synchronous and asynchronous. Do you know which is which? Put an "S" in front of the training that is synchronous, and an "A" in front of the training that is asynchronous.

1. ____ Self-paced print program to teach managers how to prepare a budget
2. ____ Live, in-person workshop on presentation skills
3. ____ Podcast on managing stress
4. ____ e-Learning program on project planning
5. ____ Virtual workshop on negotiating skills
6. ____ Study group on proposal writing
7. ____ On-the-job coaching for new executive assistant

You participated in synchronous training whenever you sat in a classroom, took a workshop, had a supervisor or colleague teach you how to do a new job, or attended a virtual (online) workshop. Synchronous training occurs when participants are all present at the same time—although not necessarily in the same location—so that they can communicate and interact with one another in real time. Synchronous training is usually, although not always, delivered by an instructor or facilitator.

Live, instructor-led workshops, in which all participants are in the same room at the same time, are the most common form of synchronous training, although many workshops include participants who attend via video or audio links. Increasingly, trainers are using "virtual" or web-based workshops, in which participants and trainers are together at the same time, but not in the same place. Study groups, in which people learn together without a facilitator or instructor, and on-the-job training or coaching, in which people learn a job by working directly with a manager, a colleague, or a coach, are other forms of synchronous training. Synchronous training is essential when learners need to share experiences, perspectives, and points of view; receive immediate feedback on their performance; improve interpersonal and communication skills; collaborate on solutions to problems; apply what they are learning to complex issues; and discuss concepts and ideas.

Asynchronous training is characterized by a lack of real-time interaction—often, no direct interaction at all—between learners and between learners and the instructor. You have participated in asynchronous training if you've taken a computer tutorial to learn a new application, used a self-study workbook to prepare for an exam, followed the instructions on a job aid to learn how to do a task, or watched a videotaped "webinar" that delivered information but offered no opportunity for real-time interaction. (You are participating in asynchronous learning by doing the exercises as you read this book.)

The content of an asynchronous training program is predetermined and static, which makes it a good way to deliver training when all the participants need to learn the same information in the same way. Learners do not need to travel or free up time to attend a workshop. They can usually choose the time and place that work best for them, and they can do as much or as little of a program at one time as they wish. A well-designed print or e-learning program includes opportunities for the practice and feedback that help people learn.

2. Characteristics of Common Delivery Methods

We've already mentioned most of the common methods of delivering training. Now let's take a closer look.

Synchronous Training

Live, Trainer-Led Classroom Training

As mentioned earlier, the great advantage of this delivery method is the opportunities it offers for the immediate, face-to-face interaction that can be so essential to learning. Another advantage, especially when training has to be delivered quickly or you are training small numbers of people, is that workshops can often be put together relatively easily and inexpensively. They also offer a great deal of flexibility—the trainer can usually update the content and customize training on the spot to meet the needs of a specific group.

But workshops are not right for every situation. They may not be the best or most cost-effective way to teach factual information or mechanical skills, for example. Workshops require learners to free up a significant block of time. Bringing widely disbursed learners together in the same place can be a logistical nightmare—and costly. Learners who must attend via a telephone or video link won't benefit from the same level of interaction as those who are in the room. Not everyone likes to learn in a group setting. And when some participants have more experience, a higher level of skills, and/or more knowledge about the subject than others do, it can be difficult to construct the workshop so that everyone finds all parts of it useful.

Live, Trainer-Led Virtual Training

Organizations are increasingly taking advantage of technology to meet the needs of participants who are widely disbursed and have limited time available for training. One solution is a virtual meeting room—a website on which an instructor and a group of participants simultaneously log on and connect with one another and the trainer via an audio link.

Virtual workshops offer opportunities for participants to interact with the trainer and with one another, although those interactions are necessarily more limited than in a "real" classroom. As in a live in-person workshop, the facilitator can explain ideas, provide information, show examples, answer questions, and lead discussions. Learners can work together in "breakout" sessions and then share their ideas or conclusions with the group.

The facilitator can provide handouts in the form of e-mail attachments; for multi-session workshops, participants can be asked to complete assignments.

The obvious advantage of virtual workshops is that people can participate from anywhere in the world, although time zones need to be considered when scheduling sessions. Virtual workshops are generally much shorter than classroom sessions, requiring participants to take smaller blocks of time away from their work.

There are a number of disadvantages as well. Designing, developing, and conducting virtual training requires both the technology and the expertise to use it. Because participants communicate with each other and the facilitator by voice, they lack the nonverbal communication that happens when people are face to face. Facilitators cannot see the participants, so they do not have the nonverbal cues that tell them whether people are interested and comprehending what they are learning—or checking their e-mail.

Virtual Worlds

Instructional designers have recently begun to use gaming technology to transform the virtual classroom into a virtual world, where learners "meet" in a realistic environment and create avatars to represent themselves when they interact with one another. In these virtual worlds, learners can explore a model, participate in a role play, or "see" one another while they hold a discussion. These virtual worlds can be extremely effective at engaging learners, stimulating their interest, encouraging them to participate in the learning process, and helping them learn through discovery and collaboration.

On-the-Job Training

My first job in high school was wrapping holiday gifts at a local men's store. How did I learn it? Another, more experienced, wrapper showed me what to do. I learned to make sharp corners on the boxes, tie three types of bows, and be friendly to the customers. That was on-the-job training, often referred to as "OJT."

You probably learned some of your jobs in much the same way. After showing you around, your manager or supervisor assigned an experienced employee to help you learn. You observed how the job was done, then tried it yourself. Your "trainer," or coach, gave you feedback, and you tried it again and again, until you had it more or less right. You might have used a job aid—instructions or a manual—to help you remember what to do. You might even have used a job aid to learn some of the tasks associated with the job, with only a little guidance from a supervisor or coach.

On-the-job training, the purest form of learning by doing, has been around ever since anyone learned to do a job. Apprenticeships in which people learn crafts such as carpentry and blacksmithing are on-the-job training. The advantages are obvious: OJT doesn't cost the organization much; it requires little, if any, preparation; the content is directly relevant; and the learning can be put to use immediately.

Clearly defined learning objectives and a program designed to meet them are just as important for OJT as for any other training. Effective on-the-job training is more than just having someone shadow an experienced worker for a couple of days. In fact, unplanned and unstructured OJT can result in performance that does not meet the organization's goals or standards.

The success of on-the-job training is also directly related to the characteristics of the designated coach—the person who is responsible for teaching the person to do the job. Whether the coach is the learner's supervisor or an experienced co-worker, he or she needs not only to understand exactly how the job is supposed to be done, but to be able to explain clearly how to do it, be patient enough to let the learner stumble through the process and make mistakes, and be able to give feedback that helps the new person learn.

Study Groups

Study groups are familiar to many of us from school, where we met with other students to prepare for exams or work together on projects. In the workplace, study groups are good ways for people to come together to learn something on their own. For example, people who are taking a self-paced print or e-learning program might meet for a couple of hours once or twice a week in person, in a web-based meeting room, or in a chat room to discuss what they are learning, do some of the program activities as a group, help one another answer questions, and explore ways to apply the learning on the job.

Study groups work best when they are small—three to ten people. Some kind of structure and oversight helps groups avoid the common tendency to fall apart or become distracted. The group should establish procedures and guidelines when they begin. Someone—perhaps each member in turn—must be responsible for scheduling, including sending out reminders. At the end of each session, participants can take a few minutes to make assignments and plan the next session.

Asynchronous Training

Self-Paced Print

I remember using a self-paced workbook to take a college course in statistics and another when I flirted with the idea of becoming a realtor. In fact, as mentioned in the Introduction to this book, I originally learned the basics of instructional design by completing a self-paced workbook. Self-paced print can be a very efficient way to deliver training to large numbers of people when the topic doesn't require much, if any, interaction with others and when it is important that everyone receive the same content in the same way. People can carry the workbooks around with them and complete the lessons, which include exercises, activities, and feedback, on their own schedule. Self-paced print programs take time and expertise to develop, but once developed, their low-tech nature makes them relatively inexpensive to produce and administer.

Until recently, a significant disadvantage to this method of delivering training was its lack of flexibility—once it was published, a self-paced print program couldn't be changed until the next printing. Today, however, self-paced workbooks can be printed on demand or delivered electronically as PDF files, which makes it easy to keep them up-to-date and to customize them for individuals and groups.

There are two remaining disadvantages to self-paced print that are important to consider when deciding whether this method might be best for a given situation. One is that, in this highly technological age, training that requires the use of paper and pencils may seem old-fashioned. The other is that, without sufficient motivation and guidance, some learners never get around to completing the program. For that reason, self-paced programs of all kinds work best when they are introduced properly, with an emphasis on the benefits of the program to the learner and to the organization, and have built-in mechanisms for providing learners with support and encouragement, feedback, and follow-up.

Self-Paced Electronic

For subjects that don't require human interaction but do require practice, e-learning—self-paced training delivered on a computer or even on a mobile device—has become one of the most popular methods of delivering training. That's not surprising: We use our computers for just about everything these days; why not for learning as well?

Well-designed e-learning programs can provide lots of the interactivity and feedback that are essential to learning. One advantage is that, as with print programs, people can take the lessons at times of their own choosing and work on the program just about anywhere—while waiting for a plane, working from home, even at the beach (not recommended). Online e-learning programs are easier to tailor to individual learners' needs and may be easier to update than print programs. If the program is delivered over an organization's intranet, a trainer or administrator can use specialized software to track usage, providing a record of learners' progress and test scores.

The most serious downside to e-learning has been the expense, the required expertise, and the development time—as long as three months for a single hour-long e-learning module. That's no longer the case. New authoring software is making it possible for people with little technical expertise to develop e-learning modules much more quickly, thus making e-learning a possible delivery option in a wider range of situations.

As with self-paced print programs, learners still need motivation to complete self-paced e-learning programs. They are more likely to find the time when they have clear objectives that are linked to their own goals and those of the organization, sufficient feedback and guidance, and follow-up.

Learning Management Systems

Technology has not only created new options for the ways in which training is delivered, but it has made it easier for organizations to manage the complexities of the training function. A learning management system (LMS) is software that can be used to register people for training programs; provide them with access to those programs and track their progress; manage training resources; collect and analyze data; facilitate planning; and more. If an organization does not have the resources or inclination to develop its own learning management system, software is available from a wide range of vendors.

Audio and Video Podcasts

I don't really consider podcasts training, because there are no exercises, no interactivity, and no feedback. But if all people need is information, why not make it available while they're on the bus, or on the treadmill at the gym? Essentially little lectures or video clips, podcasts that can be listened to or watched on a computer or a mobile electronic device give people the kinds of information they used to obtain by listening to an audiotape, reading, or attending a presentation—tips for making sales calls, managing time productively, or giving positive feedback; updates on a new product launch; demonstrations of a product or process; background information for a meeting; or pre-work for a training workshop.

Podcasts can be very inexpensive to produce and deliver, but they do require some amount of planning and expertise. To provide people with a more complete learning experience, you can combine podcasts with other training methods.

> ## Rapid e-Learning
>
> In past years, the expertise and development time required for e-learning programs have led many organizations to opt for other ways to deliver training, even when e-learning appeared to meet the needs of both the learners and the situation. That's changing. With readily available authoring software, even non-technical people can now produce good e-learning programs. By using the right software and making sure that the design and development process is as efficient as possible, organizations are increasingly able to choose e-learning as a viable option even when they have relatively low budgets and a relatively short amount of time in which to provide training.

Webinars

Like podcasts, web-based seminars or web events are more like presentations than training—there is little or no immediate interaction between the presenter and the participants or between participants. Some webinars offer the opportunity for participants to ask questions via e-mail, an audio link, or a chat, but the Q&A portion is usually limited.

In a webinar, presenters can use graphics, whiteboards, slides, and video clips and share documents, just as they would in a virtual workshop. Webinars can also be presented to audiences of any size, unlike virtual workshops in which the audience needs to be small enough so that everyone can participate. Participants can attend webinars in real time; they can also watch a recorded version of the event if they can't attend or would like to see it again.

Videos

Videos can be an excellent way to deliver information, explain concepts, demonstrate how something works, or model behavior. But to be useful as a training method, videos have to be accompanied by activities such as discussion, reflection, and practice that help people learn. Professional quality videos can be very expensive to produce, and they cannot be easily changed. But there is a vast supply of off-the-shelf videos available on a wide range of topics, and many of them come with discussion guides or trainer guides with activities so that they can be used in a workshop or a self-directed learning program.

Blended Learning

> *Blended learning is a custom approach that applies a mix of training delivery options to teach, support, and sustain the skills needed for top job performance. With blended learning, the tried-and-true traditional learning methods are combined with new technology to create a synergistic, dynamic learning structure that can propel learning to new heights.*
>
> Caroline Gray, "Blended Learning: Why Everything Old Is New Again—But Better," *ASTD Learning Circuits*, 2006

THINK ABOUT IT

Suppose you are designing a training program to help one hundred sales representatives increase their sales by making more effective product presentations to potential customers. Three of the learning objectives are to be able to (1) develop a PowerPoint slide presentation tailored to the customer's needs; (2) prepare for a presentation; and (3) deliver a presentation. What combination of training methods might the program include?

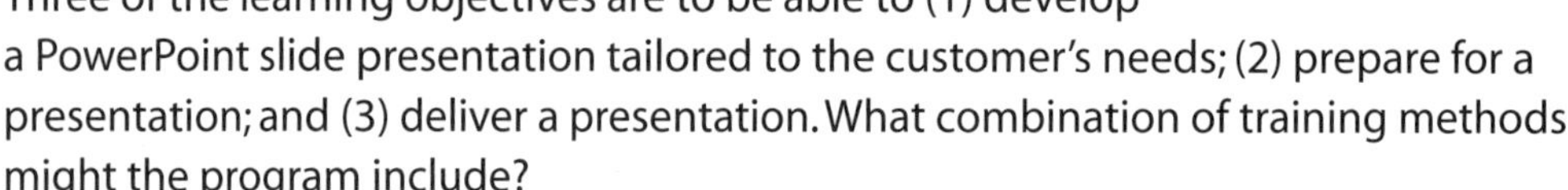

____

____

"One size fits all"—or at least it does unless your body type doesn't match the norm. That's true of training as well. Blended learning refers to the results of combining different methods to make training more closely fit the unique needs and constraints of a specific situation. This is not a new concept: classroom training has long been combined with and reinforced by self-study and on-the-job training, for example. But the technological tools currently available—and those on the horizon—offer instructional designers a variety of possibilities for combining methods to find the best ways to help people learn and transfer what they learn to the workplace.

Each of the training methods we've been discussing has its advantages and disadvantages. Combining methods helps you make the most of each method to find the most cost-effective way of putting together a program that meets both the requirements and constraints. But it's not just a matter of picking options out of a grab bag: the learning program must truly be blended so that all the parts fit together to make a cohesive whole.

Here are a few examples of ways in which you might use blended learning:

- Use podcasts to deliver information that people need to prepare for a workshop or to reinforce what they learned.
- Use a study group and online webinars to reinforce what people are learning in a self-paced e-learning program.
- Use e-mail, bulletin boards, threaded discussions, and social networking sites during or after a workshop to help learners stay in touch with one another, share ideas and best practices, and answer each other's questions.
- Use print or online self-study to support on-the-job training.
- Extend the value of a webinar by setting up a chat or discussion group with suggested discussion questions.
- Use videos for demonstrations and to trigger discussions in a workshop.
- Use virtual world technology to set up simulations that participants experience and then discuss in a live in-person or virtual workshop.

3. How to Choose a Delivery Method

THINK ABOUT IT

Below are brief descriptions of some training needs. Which of the following delivery method or methods might best meet those needs?

(A) Live, in-person workshop (B) Virtual workshop
(C) e-Learning program (D) Podcast (E) On-the-job training

1. ____ Approximately 125 mid-level managers who are located in ten different states and three different countries need training in leadership skills. The executive team wants training to be completed within twelve months.
2. ____ Approximately fifty sales associates who work in different states need to learn how to use Excel to create customer lists and track customer contacts.
3. ____ Each month, approximately five newly hired employees in the organization's customer service center need to learn how to take and process orders.
4. ____ Whenever the company updates a product, approximately one hundred sales representatives, who travel constantly, need details about the changes as quickly as possible.
5. ____ Fourteen members of a management team who work closely together at corporate headquarters need to improve the way they go about making decisions.
6. ____ A newly hired front-desk person at a software company needs to learn how to greet, sign in, and announce visitors.

Imagine that you are getting ready to buy a new car. You might be the type of person who buys on impulse: you just like the look and feel of a certain model. But to make an informed decision about which make and model will best meet your needs, you'd need to consider a lot of things, such as the initial price; cost of maintenance; potential resale value; reliability; impact on the environment; size and carrying capacity; ease of use; comfort; and your preferences in terms of color and features. Considering those factors would help you narrow the options until you found the make, model, and deal that fit your needs most closely.

Some people also choose training delivery methods on impulse—they like workshops over e-learning, or vice-versa. But just as buying a car on impulse might mean that you spend too much money for what you get, choosing a training delivery method on impulse can mean that you spend too much money on a program that doesn't accomplish its goals.

To make an informed decision about which delivery method or methods to use, you need to ask a lot of questions, drawing on the information you collected during the analysis stage and collecting more, if necessary. The answers help you narrow down the options so you can select those that are most likely to achieve the desired outcome, considering the constraints and stakeholders' preferences.

Here are some of those questions:

- *What is the training expected to accomplish?* What are the organization's goals and expectations for this program? What are the learning objectives? As you've learned throughout this book, keeping a focus on the destination helps you determine the best way to get there.
- *What do participants need to learn?* Do they need to learn or improve skills, acquire knowledge, and/or change attitudes? Different methods work best for different types of learning. Think about whether what they need to learn requires interaction or whether it lends itself to self-paced instruction. A team-building or interpersonal communication skills need a program in which people can interact; one that helps people learn how to prepare a budget could more easily be delivered in a self-paced format than in a workshop; and on-the-job training might be the best way to help a retail clerk learn how to ring up sales.
- *How many people need to be trained, and what are their responsibilities?* It would seem logical that the larger the target audience, the more likely it is

that the organization will receive a good return on its investment, because the per-person cost of training will go down. But it's also worthwhile to invest in a small group of valuable top performers by providing training that increases their ability to contribute to the organization's success and makes it more likely that they will stay. For that group, even a more expensive per-person delivery method is likely to pay off.

- *How often will the program be repeated? How likely is it to change?* General skills training programs on topics such as delegating, business writing, or running meetings might be repeated over and over for years with few changes, while training on the features of new products or procedures that are subject to change might be delivered to only a limited number of people for a limited period of time. It's probably not worthwhile to spend a great deal of money on a delivery method for a program with limited use and a limited life span, or on programs with content that is subject to frequent change.
- *What's the urgency?* When does training have to be completed? You may often be asked to put together programs to meet immediate, urgent needs. Be realistic about the kinds of delivery methods you can use when the development time is limited. Otherwise, you might find yourself turning out a half-finished, poorly thought-out program that meets no one's needs, least of all the learners.' Except for on-the-job training and study groups, which have limited uses, workshops are usually the default in those situations, partly because they do not depend on technology and specialized expertise.
- *What resources are available for this program?* The delivery method you select will always depend to some degree on the resources—budget, expertise, equipment, facilities, technology—you have available. Again, be realistic. There is no sense planning a sophisticated e-learning program if you have a severely limited budget and no in-house expertise.
- *Where are the learners?* How easily can people be brought together for training? If there isn't enough time or money to bring people together in one location, the target audience might be large enough to warrant sending a trainer around to different groups. Otherwise, you'll need to consider other options, such as a web-based workshop or e-learning supplemented by telephone and/or e-mail discussions.

- *What are the stakeholders' preferences?* Often, the key stakeholders—decision-makers, the learners' managers, or perhaps the learners themselves—express a preference for one form of training over another. To gain as much support for the program as possible, you need to take those preferences seriously. But you also need to speak up if you strongly believe that the preferred delivery method is unlikely to meet the need as well as another—and be prepared to justify your recommendation.

This table lists some potential delivery methods and some of their advantages.

Delivery Options and Considerations

Delivery Method	Good For	What to Consider
Live, trainer-led workshops	Learning that requires face-to-face interaction: discussions, collaborative learning, group projects, immediate feedback, diverse perspectives	Can be developed relatively quickly and inexpensively; cost-effective way to train small groups; can easily be tailored to group needs; learners and trainer must be in same location at same time
Live trainer-led virtual training	Learning that requires real-time interaction when learners and trainer cannot be in same place at same time	Requires expertise and technology; trainer and participants cannot obtain visual cues from one another; must be presented in shorter modules than in-person workshops; can be taped for later viewing; can be tailored to group needs
Self-paced print	Training large numbers of people when real-time interaction and one-on-one feedback aren't necessary	Can be developed relatively inexpensively; works best when accompanied by support structure; may seem old-fashioned to younger workers; may be difficult to update or tailor to learners' needs
Self-paced electronic	Learning that doesn't require real-time interaction with other people but does require practice and feedback	Can be costly and time-consuming to develop; works best when accompanied by support structure; can be appealing to learners who use technology every day; can be designed with flexibility in mind; can be set up to track the learner's progress

(*Continued*)

Delivery Options and Considerations (*Continued*)

Delivery Method	Good For	What to Consider
Webinar or web event	Learning doesn't require practice, feedback, or real-time interaction with trainer or other participants	Requires technical expertise to use the software; can be used with infinitely large audiences; used alone, may enhance knowledge but not necessarily promote learning
Podcast	Delivery of information when feedback, interaction, and practice are not necessary	Used alone, may enhance knowledge but not necessarily promote learning; can be used with other training methods to provide a more complete learning experience; easy to use; relatively easy and inexpensive to produce and to change
Videos	Delivery of information and for demonstrations when feedback, interaction, and practice are not necessary	Used alone, may enhance knowledge but not necessarily promote learning; can be used with other training methods to provide more complete learning experience; can be expensive to produce and change
Study groups	Helping learners support and reinforce one another while they participate in another form of training	Learners can meet in person or in a virtual meeting room; relatively low cost; requires some administration, which can come from the group
On-the-job training	Helping people learn by doing the job under guidance of an experienced person	Relatively low cost; directly relevant training; provides learner with feedback and practice; requires a knowledgeable, competent coach
Blended learning	Combining methods to meet specific needs in a cost-effective way	Must be planned carefully so that all the methods work together well; can provide the interaction and feedback missing from self-paced learning, podcasts, or videos alone; helps use valuable "real time" training more efficiently

Questions to Ask When Selecting Delivery Methods

- What is the training expected to accomplish?
- What do participants need to learn? Do they need to learn or improve skills, acquire knowledge, and/or change attitudes?
- How many people need to be trained? What are their responsibilities?
- How often will the program will be repeated? How likely is it to change?
- What's the urgency? When does training need to be completed?
- What budget, expertise, equipment, facilities, and technology are available for this program?
- Where are the learners? How easily can be they brought together for training?
- What are the stakeholders' preferences?

Boris and Marietta's Progress

Boris and Marietta considered the pros and cons of several delivery methods for the e-mail training program. "How about a self-paced program?" Boris suggested. "We could probably find a good off-the-shelf self-paced workbook on writing better e-mail—maybe even an e-learning program."

"Self-paced might be great for basic writing skills," Marietta said, "but we want this group to understand how their use of e-mail impacts our customer relationships, their ability to achieve their own goals, their teams' productivity—and the company's bottom line. I think there would be real value in building this program to meet their needs and including lots of opportunities for them to discuss issues and learn from one another."

"You're right," Boris said. "And there are two other reasons to provide training in a workshop. First, the CEO would prefer a workshop...."

"Good reason," Marietta replied.

"...and she wants the training pretty quickly. There's not really enough time—or money—to develop self-paced training, or even to find an existing program and adapt it to meet all our needs." Marietta agreed. "A workshop it is. Now....What do we do next?"

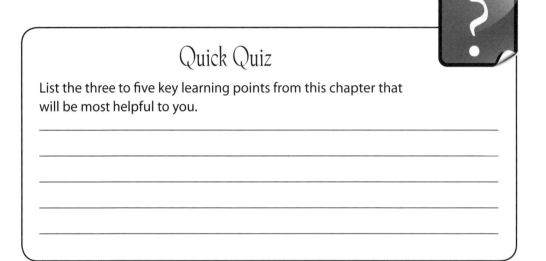

Quick Quiz

List the three to five key learning points from this chapter that will be most helpful to you.

____

____

____

____

____

What's Next?

Once you've selected a delivery option, you're ready to design and develop the content, structure, and materials for your training program. In the following chapters we'll focus on developing a workshop. But nearly everything you learn is also applicable to the design and development of e-learning and other types of programs.

Apply What You Learn

Complete the worksheet on page 123 to determine what delivery method or methods would be most appropriate, practical, and cost-effective for your training program.

Answers to Exercises

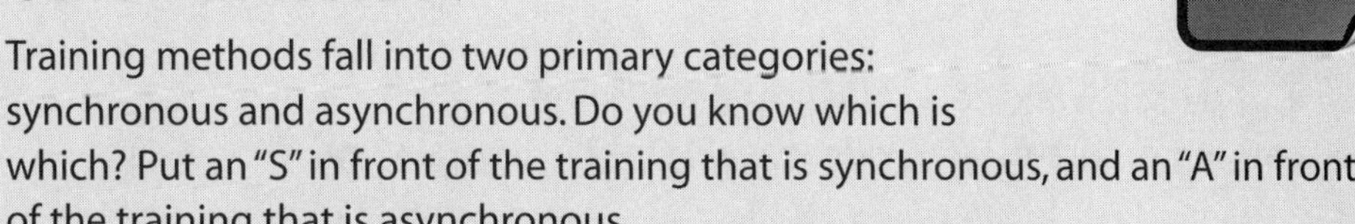

Check What You Know

Training methods fall into two primary categories: synchronous and asynchronous. Do you know which is which? Put an "S" in front of the training that is synchronous, and an "A" in front of the training that is asynchronous.

1. __A__Self-paced print program to teach managers how to prepare a budget
2. __S__ Live, in-person workshop on presentation skills
3. __A__ Podcast on managing stress
4. __A__ e-Learning program on project planning
5. S, A__ Virtual workshop on negotiating skills
6. __S__ Study group on proposal writing
7. __S__ On-the-job coaching for new executive assistant

THINK ABOUT IT

Below are brief descriptions of some training needs. Which of the following delivery method or methods might best meet those needs?

(A) Live, in-person workshop (B) Virtual workshop
(C) e-Learning program (D) Podcast (E) On-the-job training

1. __A, B__ Approximately 125 mid-level managers who are located in ten different states and three different countries need training in leadership skills. The executive team wants training to be completed within twelve months.
2. __C__ Approximately fifty sales associates who work in different states need to learn how to use Excel to create customer lists and track customer contacts.
3. _C, E_ Each month, approximately five newly hired employees in the organization's customer service center need to learn how to take and process orders.
4. __D__ Whenever the company updates a product, approximately one hundred sales representatives, who travel constantly, need details about the changes as quickly as possible.
5. __A__ Fourteen members of a management team who work closely together at corporate headquarters need to improve the way they go about making decisions.
6. __E__ A newly hired front-desk person at a software company needs to learn how to greet, sign in, and announce visitors.

Worksheet

Selecting the Delivery Method

Topic: ____

____

Intended goals: ____

____

____

Brief description of target audience: ______________________________

____

____

1. What do participants need to learn?
   - ❑ Learn or improve skills
   - ❑ Acquire knowledge
   - ❑ Change attitudes

   To what degree does what they need to learn require collaboration and interaction?

   ____

   ____

   How many people need to be trained? ______________________
   What are their responsibilities?

   ____

   ____

(*Continued*)

How often will the program will be repeated?

____

How likely is the program to change?

- ❑ Very likely
- ❑ Possibly
- ❑ Not likely

When does training need to be completed? ________________

2. What resources are available for this program?

   - Budget: ________________
   - Expertise: ________________
   - Equipment: ________________
   - Facilities: ________________
   - Technology: ________________
   - Other: ________________

3. Where are the learners?

   - ❑ All in the same location
   - ❑ In different locations
   - ❑ Widely disbursed

   What would bringing the learners together for training involve?

   ____

4. Have any stakeholders expressed a preference for a delivery method? If yes, which stakeholders? Which delivery method do they prefer?

   Stakeholder: ______________ Delivery preference: ______________

   Stakeholder: ______________ Delivery preference: ______________

   Stakeholder: ______________ Delivery preference: ______________

5. What other factors need to be considered when selecting a delivery option?

   ____

   ____

   ____

   ____

   ____

6. What delivery option or options would best meet the needs of the learners and the situation?

   - ❑ Live, in-person workshop
   - ❑ Virtual workshop
   - ❑ e-Learning
   - ❑ Self-paced print
   - ❑ Study group
   - ❑ On-the-job training
   - ❑ Other (describe)

   ____

   ____

   ____

   ____

   ____

   ____

5
Identifying Content

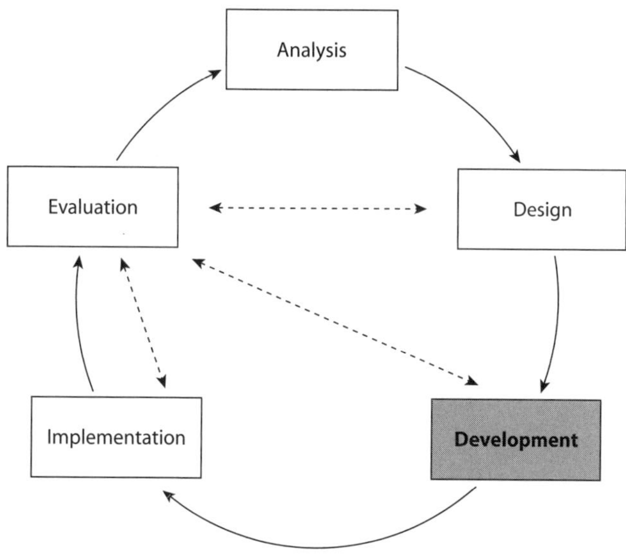

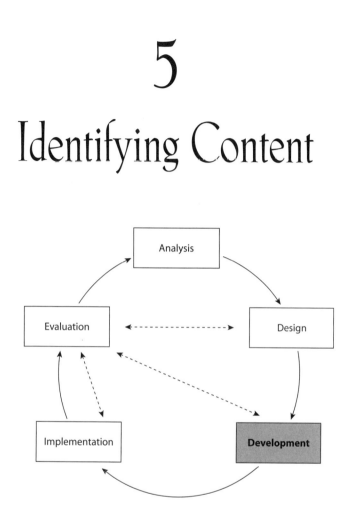

The Development Stage of the ADDIE Model

Check What You Know

After evaluating all the options, Boris and Marietta decided that a workshop would be the best way to deliver the e-mail training. Now they are ready to focus on the content—what people will learn in the workshop.

"We've sure got a lot of information," Marietta said as they looked over the data, ideas, suggestions, comments, and best practices they'd collected from reading the sample e-mail messages, conducting surveys, and interviews, and reading up on the subject. "I don't see how we can cover all of it in one workshop."

Boris agreed. "But how are we going to decide what's important and what's not?"

If you were advising Boris and Marietta at this stage of their project, what advice would you give them? What do they need to think about when deciding what content to include? How can they go about the process of making that important decision?

____

____

____

____

____

____

When my daughter was preparing for college, we visited a large public university in Southern California. The student who led the tour took us into a huge lecture hall where he described a course given by a well-regarded professor. "She's an excellent teacher," he said. "She's very detailed and thorough—her lectures are packed full of information. And when she can't be here in person, she tapes her lectures so the students don't have to miss anything." But lecturing isn't teaching, I thought. Lecturing is…lecturing. Teacher active, audience passive. Lots of content, little or no interaction. Seeing the perplexed look on my face, my daughter threw me an unmistakable signal, and I kept my mouth shut. But the next time I designed a training program, I thought back to that moment. It was a good reminder to keep the focus on what people needed to know, instead of what I wanted to say.

In this chapter, you'll learn how to:

- Use a learner-centered approach to content
- Discriminate between nice-to-know and must-know content
- Identify the content to include

Our thinking about content has long been dominated by one assumption: more is better.

Maryellen Weimer,
Learner-Centered Teaching

1. A Learner-Centered Approach to Content

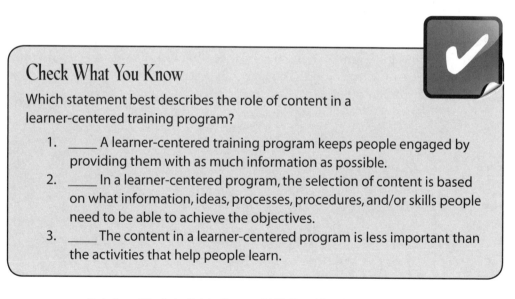

Check What You Know

Which statement best describes the role of content in a learner-centered training program?

1. ____ A learner-centered training program keeps people engaged by providing them with as much information as possible.
2. ____ In a learner-centered program, the selection of content is based on what information, ideas, processes, procedures, and/or skills people need to be able to achieve the objectives.
3. ____ The content in a learner-centered program is less important than the activities that help people learn.

To put it as simply as possible, content is what people learn in a training program. Content includes facts, concepts, processes, procedures, skills, rules, guidelines, techniques, best practices—everything that people need to learn so they can achieve the objectives.

Educator and author Maryellen Weimer explains that "the need to cover content strongly influences, if not dictates, most instructional decisions." Even when instructors know that there is too much content, Dr. Weimer goes on to say, they have difficulty leaving anything out. We've all experienced the results of this kind of teacher-centered teaching. Many of our college classes, and far too many of the training programs we've attended, have been crammed so full of content that we were lucky if we could remember the name of the course when it was over.

Although Dr. Weimer's book, *Learner-Centered Teaching*, was written for people in higher education, the learner-centered approach she presents is even more applicable to training. While a teacher-centered approach focuses on providing content that the course developer or instructor thinks that learners need, a learner-centered approach is guided by a single key question: What exactly do learners need to know?

As Boris and Marietta discovered, the challenge is how to decide what to include and what to leave out. In fact, the content for a successful training program should conform to the Goldilocks rule: not too much, not too little, but just the right amount—all the content that learners need, and only that content, not all the content that the instructional designer or trainer would like them to have.

But how do you sort through all the content that *could* be included to identify what is "just right"? In my experience, there's only one way to do that: Focus on the learning objectives. The learning objectives form the basis for deciding what content to include.

2. Nice-to-Know vs. Must-Know Content

Check What You Know

You are designing a training program to help high school graduates apply for a job. One of the learning objectives is to be able to fill out a job application. Which of the content described below do you think learners *must* know to be able to achieve that objective?

1. ____ What a correctly completed job application looks like.
2. ____ Statistics about the numbers of people hired by various industries in a given month.
3. ____ Reasons for completing job applications correctly.

It might be nice for the learners in the job application workshop to know various industries' hiring statistics, but that information does nothing to help them fill out a job application. Knowing the reasons for completing an application correctly might help prepare them to learn. But to be able to fill out an application correctly, they first need to know what a correctly completed application looks like.

During the process of designing and developing any training program, you will make countless decisions about what content to include and what to leave out. It's like deciding what to pack for a trip—the first step is to think about where you're going and what you're going to do when you get there. Do you really need that heavy jacket? Those formal evening clothes? Five pairs of shoes? After lugging too many suitcases through too many airports, most experienced travelers learn to pack as lightly as possible. In the same way, experienced instructional designers follow the excellent advice that an expert in the field gave me when I began designing training programs: "Keep it lean." Just as packing lightly means packing only what you really need, keeping a training program lean means including only the content that is necessary for learners to achieve the objectives, and for the program to achieve the desired outcome:

Desired outcome ➔ learning objectives and enabling objectives ➔ **content**

3. How to Identify Content

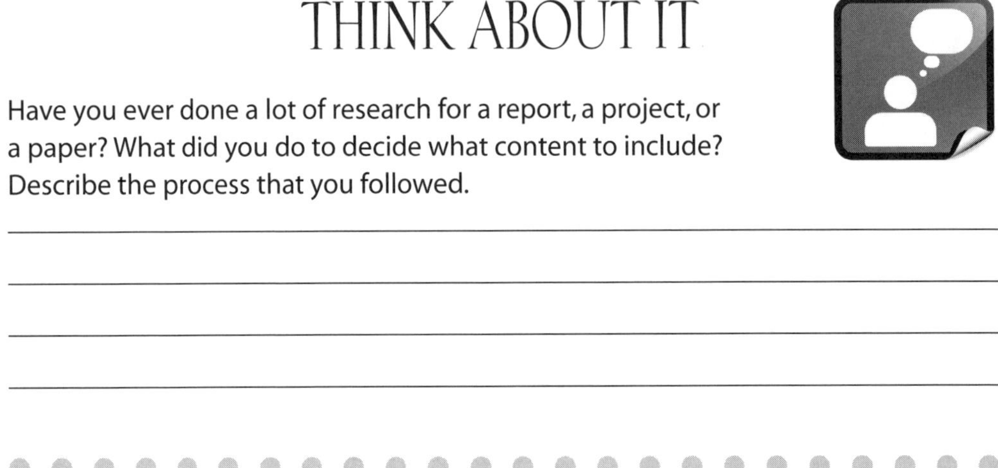

THINK ABOUT IT

Have you ever done a lot of research for a report, a project, or a paper? What did you do to decide what content to include? Describe the process that you followed.

Life—and work—is always easier when there is a clear right way to do something. But like so much else in training, there is no perfect method for selecting the content to include in a training program. Some instructional designers select the content before choosing the learning activities, some design or select the activities before identifying the content, and many swing back and forth between those tasks, looking for activities to teach specific content and content that people need to be able to do specific activities. (You'll learn more about selecting activities in the next chapter.)

Below, I've described a process for selecting the content that you can adapt in a way that works for you. The examples are drawn from the job application training discussed in Chapter 4. The process starts with the information gathered during the analysis stage of ADDIE and draws on work that was done to identify the learning objectives.

1. Focus on the overall goal of the training program—the desired outcome. You might even want to write that goal on a Post-it Note and keep it in front of you while you work.

Example: For the job application program, the goal is to provide high school graduates with information and skills they need to look for a job.

2. Think about the target audience. You've gathered a lot of information about the learners. Reviewing that information will help you decide what content the program needs to include.

   Example: Based on the results of a questionnaire that the learners completed when they registered for the workshop, about 60 percent of the students have worked at summer and after-school jobs, but the rest have never held a job before. They all signed up for the workshop voluntarily, although at least 35 percent were strongly encouraged to do so by their parents or high school counselors. Their graduating grade point averages ranged from C– to A, which indicates that they know how to learn. They are all looking for full-time jobs, even those who plan to go to college in the future. Although they have spent twelve years in school, they have little, if any, experience with training.

3. Review what the participants will already know when they come to training—their prior knowledge provides the starting place for what they need to learn. What do they already know about the subject of job hunting? What skills do they already have? What preconceptions or attitudes are they likely to have toward the subject and the learning process? At this stage, you might find that you need to make certain assumptions about the audience and/or stop and gather more information.

   Example: Their questionnaires indicate that nearly two-thirds of the students learned something about the job application process in high school, but none have applied the process to the search for a permanent, full-time job. It's safe to assume that they all know what a job application is and understand that the application process will include an interview. They probably have a limited understanding of the kinds of information they will be expected to provide on an application, the questions they may need to answer during an interview, and the role that behavior and appearance play in hiring decisions. Their responses to the questionnaire indicate that most of them feel some anxiety about the process and about entering the workforce, and many have unrealistic expectations about the kind of job for which they are qualified.

4. Select one learning objective and the related enabling objectives to focus on. Ask, "What do learners need to know and be able to do to

achieve this learning objective?" Write down everything that occurs to you, without stopping to evaluate, criticize, or organize the points. (A whiteboard or a flip-chart page can be helpful.) This is a brainstorming process—keep going until you seem to have run out of ideas. When you reach a stopping point, you might want to take a break and then come back to your list and ask the question again.

As you work, remain alert for signs that you need to revise or even eliminate or add an objective. You might realize that learners already know most of what they need to know to achieve a specific objective, so the objective isn't really necessary, or you might see that what appeared to be a learning objective is really an enabling objective for another learning objective. You might find that an objective is lacking necessary standards or conditions. You might even find that what appeared to be one learning objective is really two. Make any necessary changes before proceeding.

Example: One of the job-seekers' learning objectives is to be able to be able to complete a job application correctly. Here's a preliminary list of what they might need to know (this is only an example, so it's not a complete list):

Objective: Given a job description and an application form, complete the application accurately and completely.

Learners need to know:

- What different types of application forms look like
- What a correctly completed application looks like
- The purpose of the application
- Why applications need to be complete and correct
- What to do if they don't understand or can't answer a question
- How companies evaluate applications
- What companies are looking for in an application
- The kinds of information an application asks for
- The importance of writing neatly and legibly
- What kind of pen to use
- Computer-based job applications
- Why it's important to be truthful and accurate
- The role the application plays in the hiring process

5. Step back and examine what you've written, looking for themes, natural groupings, and key topics. Mark up your list, circling or highlighting the key topics, crossing out redundancies or unnecessary items, adding necessary items, and connecting subtopics to topics. Then recopy the list to show the key topics and related subtopics for each learning objective. If, at this point, you have any activities in mind, indicate them at the appropriate places.

   Example:

Objective: Given a job description and an application form, complete the application accurately and completely.

- How companies evaluate job applications (Activities: examples; group discussion—employer's point of view)
- What employers are looking for
- Why applications need to be complete, correct, neat, and legible
- Why it's important to be truthful and accurate
- The kinds of information an application needs to include (Activity: group discussion)
  - Personal
  - Work experience
  - Education
  - Other relevant experience
  - What applications should not include
  - Completing an application (examples; practice)
  - Different types of applications
  - A correctly completed application
  - Computer-based applications
  - What to do if you can't answer a question

6. Repeat the process for each of the remaining learning objectives.

Mind Mapping

Information mapping, or mind mapping, is a brainstorming technique that can help you sort through lots of content quickly. Some people find it more useful than making a linear list. Here's one way to use it:

Make a circle in the center of a piece of paper, a whiteboard, or a flip-chart page. Write a learning objective in the circle.

(*Continued*)

Around the circle, write down everything learners need to know or be able to do to achieve that objective. Put a circle around each item and connect the circles with lines to show the relationships between them. Combine items, cross out redundant and nice-to-know items, and add others that you think are necessary.

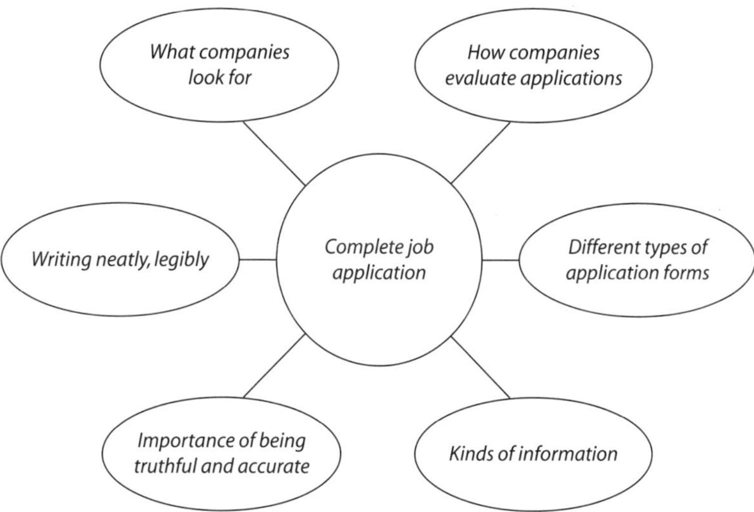

By the time you've finished the "map," you'll have a pretty good idea of what content to include for that learning objective. Repeat the process for the rest of the learning objectives and you'll have identified the content for your program.

By the time you have reached this point, you will have a pretty good idea about how your program will be organized, and you will probably have a preliminary outline. Before you finish the outline, however, you need to select the activities. You'll learn how to do that in Chapter 6. In Chapter 7, you'll how to pull everything together into a logical sequence, with the content and activities in the best order to help people learn.

Suggested Working Process for Identifying Content

1. Think about the desired outcome and the learners' characteristics.
2. Consider what the learners already know.
3. List everything learners need to know and be able to do to achieve one of the learning objective and the related enabling objective.
4. Look for themes, natural groupings, and key topics.
5. Copy the list into a rough content outline, noting possible activities.
6. Repeat the process for each of the other learning objectives and the related enabling objectives.

Another Way to Identify Content

Instead of starting by thinking about the target audience and the learning objectives, you might prefer to start by brainstorming a list of everything you think that the program should cover to achieve the desired outcome. Once your list seems to be complete, go over the items and link each one to a learning objective. Cross out items that do not accurately represent what learners need to know and add anything else that seems to be necessary for learners to achieve a specific objective. If you think something is necessary but it doesn't link clearly to a learning objective, consider whether you might need to add an objective.

THINK ABOUT IT

Below is another objective for the job search training program. What do learners need to know and be able to do to achieve this objective? List everything you can think of. Then use a separate sheet of paper (or your computer) to revise the list and identify the topics and subtopics to include.

Objective: Given a job description and a completed application form, interview for a job.

Content:

What If There's Too Much Content—Or Too Little?

Sometimes you will discover that you have too much content that needs to be included; occasionally, you'll find that you don't have enough content to fill the time. Here are some suggestions for handling both situations:

(*Continued*)

Too Much Content

- Meet with the decision-makers and other stakeholders to find out whether it is possible to extend the length of the training program. For example, if you are planning a one-day workshop, see whether it's possible to extend the workshop to two days. Be prepared to explain how the additional time will benefit the learners and the organization.
- If the program length cannot be extended, work with the stakeholders to revise the program goals and decide what learning objectives are most important. Help them understand that trying to squeeze too much into limited time is unlikely to result in a program that achieves the desired outcomes.
- Consider splitting off some objectives into another program. Examine the objectives and the related content to see whether there is a logical split so that the program can be easily divided.

Too Little Content

- Review the desired outcome and all the learning objectives again. Make sure that you haven't left out a learning objective or missed important content for one or more of the objectives. Also check to see whether you have inadvertently combined two objectives into one.
- Make sure that you have enough information. You might need to stop at this point so that you can collect more.
- Talk with the stakeholders about whether the program needs to be as long as it was originally planned. Perhaps the goal can be achieved in less workshop time or fewer self-paced modules.
- Think about whether achieving the goal really requires the type of training program you are developing. If the objectives are not as difficult to achieve as you originally thought, perhaps the outcome can be achieved in a less complicated way.

Boris and Marietta's Progress

Focusing on the desired outcome, the target audience, the learning objectives and the enabling objectives, made it easy for Boris and Marietta to make decisions about what content to include and what to leave out.

But reviewing the content list they generated, Marietta frowned. "This is an awful lot to cover," she said. "If we try to include everything here, the workshop's going to be two or three days long. I don't think that people will be able to take that much time away from work, do you?"

"Probably not," Boris said. "Maybe we have to re-think the objectives."

They went over the objectives again. After a few minutes, Marietta said, "Does this program really have to teach people how to use language and grammar?"

"There were lots of errors in the sample e-mails, and that was one of the CEO's concerns," Boris said.

"But there really isn't enough time to cover that content in any depth. And not everyone needs it."

"How about this," Boris suggested. "We remove that objective from the program. We can point out the importance of writing correctly and give people some resources for learning how to do that. Then we recommend that the company provide a separate training program on language and grammar for the people who need it."

"Excellent idea," Marietta said.

Using the revised objectives, here is a look at the content that Boris and Marietta came up with, along with a few activities they thought they might use:

- Standards for the use of e-mail (Activity: group discussion—"give advice to a new colleague about using e-mail")
    - Consequences of sloppy, error-filled, inappropriate, unnecessary messages
    - Account Services e-mail policies

- Appropriate content for e-mail
    - What's not appropriate (confidential, sensitive, offensive)
    - Determining whether e-mail is appropriate choice for a specific message
- Getting the message across (group or individual activity and practice)
    - Reader's point of view
    - Primary purpose—to inform or to influence
    - Clear, concise statement that expresses most important point(s)
- Including the right information and organizing it logically (group or individual activity and practice)
    - How to identify readers' questions
    - Organizing information so it's easy to follow
    - When and how to use headings and subheadings
    - When and how to use attachments
- Using the right tone (discuss examples)
    - Importance of tone
    - Factors that affect tone
- Determining who should receive an e-mail message
    - Primary and secondary readers
    - Distribution lists
- Writing subject lines
    - Criteria for a useful subject line
- Managing e-mail time (activity: assess use of time)
    - How to reduce e-mail interruptions
    - How to end an e-mail "conversation"
- Closing activity: Write set of guidelines for using e-mail for your team

Quick Quiz

List the three to five key learning points from this chapter that will be most helpful to you.

____

____

____

____

____

What's Next?

People learn, remember, and are able to use content far better if they interact with it during training. In the next chapter, you'll learn how to select activities that help participants learn the content and use what they learn after training has been completed.

Apply What You Learn

Complete the worksheet on the last page of the chapter to select the content to include for one of the learning objectives for your training program. Repeat the process for each of the remaining objectives until you have a workable content outline.

Answers to Exercises

Check What You Know

Which statement best describes the role of content in a learner-centered training program?

1. ___ A learner-centered training program keeps people engaged by providing them with as much information as possible.
2. _X_ In a learner-centered program, the selection of content is based on what information, ideas, processes, procedures, and/or skills people need to be able to achieve the objectives.
3. ___ The content in a learner-centered program is less important than the activities that help people learn.

Check What You Know

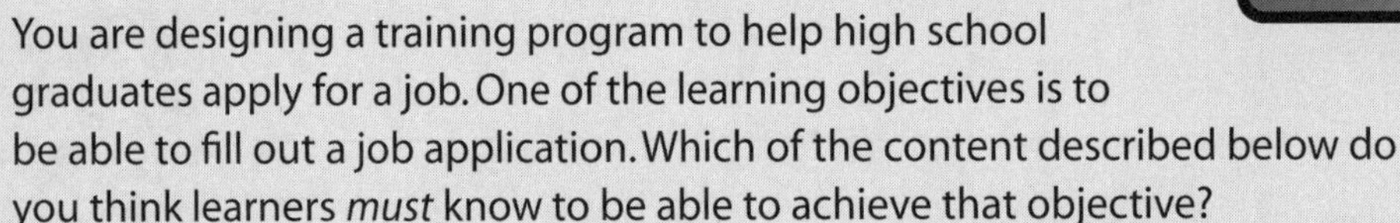

You are designing a training program to help high school graduates apply for a job. One of the learning objectives is to be able to fill out a job application. Which of the content described below do you think learners *must* know to be able to achieve that objective?

1. _X_ What a correctly completed job application looks like.
2. ___ Statistics about the numbers of people hired by various industries in a given month.
3. ___ Reasons for completing job applications correctly.

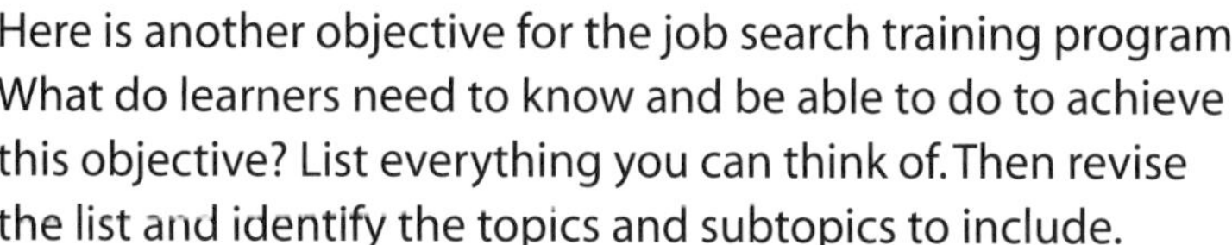

THINK ABOUT IT

Here is another objective for the job search training program. What do learners need to know and be able to do to achieve this objective? List everything you can think of. Then revise the list and identify the topics and subtopics to include.

Objective: Given a job description and a completed application form, interview for a job.

Content: *Here are examples of some of the content you might have come up with.*

- *The kinds of questions interviewers are likely to ask*
- *The importance of answering questions clearly, succinctly, and accurately*
- *What to do if a question is not clear*
- *The importance of behavior and appearance*
- *What to wear to a job interview*
- *What questions to ask of an interviewer*

Worksheet

Identifying Content

Title of Training Program: ______________________

Topic of Training Program: ______________________

1. Think back to the overall goal of the training program. What's the desired outcome?

____

____

____

____

2. What do you know about the target audience that will affect the content you include?

____

____

____

____

3. What is the learners' starting place? What knowledge and skills—and attitudes—are they likely to bring to the workshop? Do you need more information about them before continuing?

____

____

____

____

4. Using a separate sheet of paper or on your computer, choose one learning objective and its related enabling objectives. Write down everything the learners need to know and be able to do to achieve this objective. When you're done, examine what you've written, looking for themes, natural groupings, and key topics. Circle or highlight key topics, cross out redundancies or points that learners really do not need to know, and connect subtopics to topics. Add any other points that occur to you.

5. Recopy your list to show the topics and subtopics for the learning objective. If you have activities in mind, indicate them at the appropriate places.

6. Repeat Steps 4 and 5 for the remaining learning and enabling objectives.

6

Planning the Learning Activities

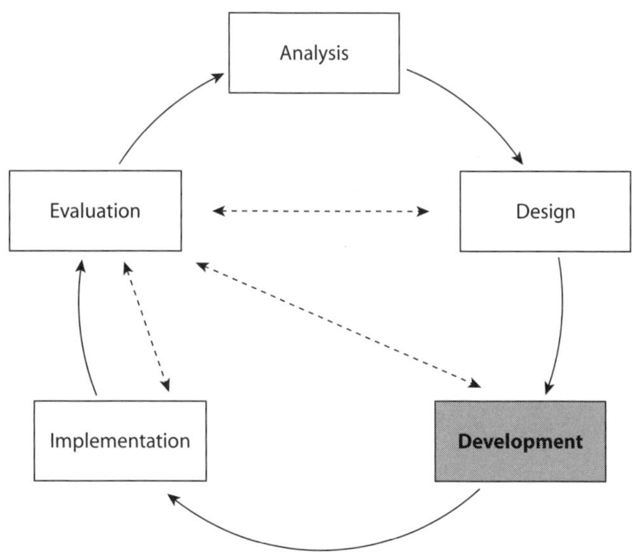

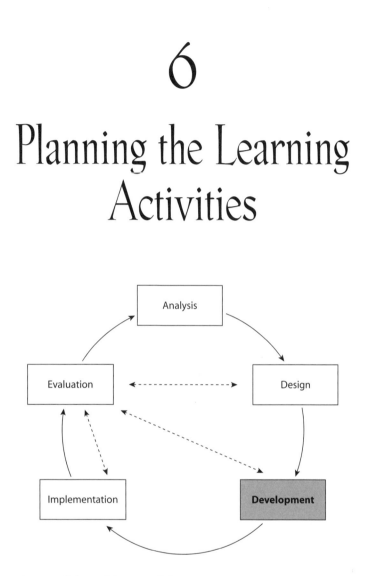

Development Stage of the ADDIE Model

Check What You Know

Boris and Marietta have been thinking about activities for the e-mail workshop. They want to focus on activities that will engage the participants and help them learn the content so they can achieve the learning objectives. Marietta has spent the morning reading through books on training and Boris has just done a web search. They meet in Marietta's office to discuss what they've found.

"I can't believe how many different kinds of activities there are," Marietta says, gesturing to a stack of books on her desk.

"And my web search came up with hundreds of suggestions—icebreakers, games, simulations, brainstorming, experiential learning, role plays—how in the world are we supposed to choose?"

How, indeed? What are some things that Boris and Marietta should consider when choosing activities for the e-mail workshop? What are some activities they might use?

____

____

____

____

____

____

A friend of mine who is a "foodie" was very excited about attending an expensive cooking course where the instructors were well-known chefs. Always wanting to be of service, I offered to let him try out what he learned on me. But the first meal was not what either he or I had hoped for. To tell the truth, we both agreed that it was pretty bad. The appetizers fell apart, the salad was soggy, the cut of meat he had special-ordered from the butcher was dry, and the dessert . . . enough said. "I'm sorry," he apologized as we scraped the plates into the garbage disposal. "It looked so easy when the chefs showed us how to make those dishes. I guess I just need more practice."

My friend had had an experience that is common to training. He left the cooking course with some excellent menus and some good ideas, but he hadn't really learned how to do anything. Experts in adult learning agree: Activities that involve and engage learners, help them draw on what they already know, and give them opportunities to practice are essential for learning.

In this chapter you'll learn about:

- Factors that affect your choice of learning activities
- Components of an experiential learning activity
- Types of activities

Engaging . . . means not only engagement between learners and facilitators and learners with each other but also the more subtle and more potent aspect of engagement, engagement between the learner and the content. . . . It is the designer's task to find ways to invite learners to dance with the new content, to engage the two realities, the personal and the new, so that real learning can take place . . . to create activities that bring the experience of the learner and the new content face to face.

Michael Milano,
"Creating Sacred Space," in T.L. Gargiulo, A.M. Pangarkar, and T. Kirkwood (Eds.),
The Trainer's Portable Mentor

1. What to Consider About Activities

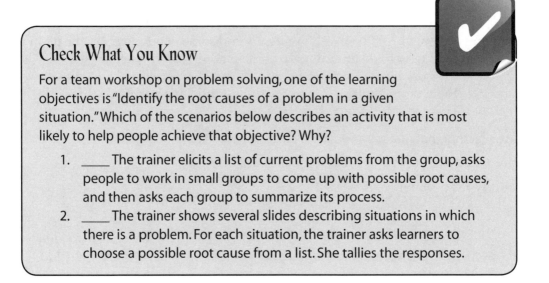

Check What You Know

For a team workshop on problem solving, one of the learning objectives is "Identify the root causes of a problem in a given situation." Which of the scenarios below describes an activity that is most likely to help people achieve that objective? Why?

1. ____ The trainer elicits a list of current problems from the group, asks people to work in small groups to come up with possible root causes, and then asks each group to summarize its process.
2. ____ The trainer shows several slides describing situations in which there is a problem. For each situation, the trainer asks learners to choose a possible root cause from a list. She tallies the responses.

Activities that are relevant and challenging engage people in the learning process and help them achieve the objectives. The best activities help people relate what they are learning to what they already know, get them thinking and reflecting, help them learn through discovery and from one another, provide opportunities for practice, and increase their ability to transfer the learning to their real world. That's why working with others to find the root causes of an existing problem and then reflecting on the process would be more likely to help people achieve the objective than would simply identifying possible root causes for problems on a list.

An activity can be as simple as a set of questions that make a lecture more interactive or a small group discussion on a given topic or as complex as a lengthy simulation in which learners experience a work-related situation, analyze that experience, and figure out how to apply what they learned. As Boris and Marietta found, a survey of training books and websites will give you hundreds, if not thousands, of activities to choose from. (Later in this chapter you'll find a discussion of the different types.)

The challenge for an instructional designer is to resist the temptation to include activities just because they are "fun" or add variety to the program. Every activity should have a clear purpose that is directly related to a learning or enabling objective. No matter how enjoyable they might be, activities that aren't relevant and do not help people achieve the objectives are not only a waste of valuable training time, but they can leave learners dissatisfied because they haven't accomplished anything.

There's a lot to consider when deciding which activities to use. Some activities are more effective than others for different types of learning and for different types of learners. Practical factors, such as budget, space, time, and group size, affect your choice of activities. Where an activity falls in terms of the time of day and the flow of the workshop can also help determine its effectiveness.

Here are some of the factors to consider when deciding which activities will best help people learn.

- *The type of learning*. Remember the KSAs—Knowledge, Skills, and Attitude—that you learned about in Chapter 3? Some activities are more useful for helping people increase their knowledge, some for helping them learn new skills or improving skills they already have, and some for helping to change their attitudes. For example, a game based on "Concentration" or a crossword puzzle might be a good way to help people learn new terminology or rules (knowledge); a role-playing activity could provide practice in using active listening techniques, closing a sale, or giving feedback (skills); and a simulated customer experience might help learners improve their understanding of how customers want to be treated (attitudes).
- *The type of knowledge*. When selecting activities, it can help to understand whether you are helping people learn *about* something or *how to do* something. These two categories of knowledge are referred to as "declarative" and "procedural."
- *Declarative* knowledge includes facts, concepts, and principles. Examples include a set of rules for a sport; the characteristics of different garden plants; and the effects of rude behavior on customer loyalty. *Procedural* knowledge is "how-to" knowledge, such as how to prepare a budget, bake a cake, change a tire, write a proposal, troubleshoot equipment problems, handle a customer complaint, or facilitate a meeting. Some examples of activities for various types of learning are given in the table on the next page.

Activities for Different Types of Learning

Type of Learning	Examples of Activities
Acquire Knowledge	Lectures or interactive lectures; panel discussions; drills and games; demonstrations; podcasts and videos
Develop Skills	Observation or demonstration followed by practice and feedback; role plays; games; simulations
Change Attitudes	Discussions; self-assessments; reflective activities; experiential activities; simulations; role plays; case studies; videos

Teaching Procedural vs. Declarative Knowledge

Wellesley Foshay, Kenneth Silber, and Michael Stelnicki, the authors of *Writing Training Materials That Work,* explain that an understanding of the distinction between the procedural and declarative knowledge helps trainers avoid certain kinds of mistakes when they design training programs. Those mistakes include:

- Using strategies best suited for teaching declarative knowledge to teach procedural knowledge, and vice versa. For example, a game that helps people memorize the steps in the procedure for processing a loan application doesn't do much to help them actually process an application; a more useful activity would be one in which they used a job aid to go through the processing steps.
- Teaching only declarative knowledge, assuming that once people understand something, they will be able to use that knowledge to do something. Being able to read and understand a recipe for apple pie doesn't ensure that the person will actually be able to make the pie (at least not so it is edible).
- Teaching only procedural knowledge, without providing people with the necessary facts, concepts, or principles. Just knowing how to carry out the tasks involved in delivering performance appraisals doesn't mean that a manager will be able—or willing—to deliver appraisals that are useful to the employee and the organization.

- *The purpose of the activity*. Make sure you know exactly what you expect each activity to achieve. With only a few exceptions, each of the activities in a training program should be intended to help learners achieve a specific learning or enabling objective. The exceptions are opening activities that are intended to help people get to know one another, feel comfortable in the workshop, develop a sense of trust, and start thinking about what they're going to learn, and closing activities that are designed to help people carry what they learn into their real worlds. If you can't come up with a relevant purpose, leave the activity out, no matter how interesting and fun it might be.
- *Available resources and time*. Some excellent activities require outdoor space, breakout rooms, computers, materials, props, assessment instruments, or other resources that might not be readily available or that would strain the budget; others take a lot of time to set up and do properly. Be realistic about the types of activities that will work within the constraints of the situation. Keep in mind that simple activities requiring few resources are often just as effective—sometimes even more effective—than those that are more complex, costly, and time-consuming. When considering lengthy, complicated activities, ask yourself whether there might be an easier way to achieve the same goal.
- *Relevance*. The more an activity relates to what people actually do on the job, the higher their level of interest and the greater the chance that they will be able to use what they learn. For example, learners will get more out of applying problem-solving techniques to a real, existing problem than to a made-up problem to which they cannot easily relate.
- *Trainer qualifications*. Some activities, such as certain simulations and outdoor experiential learning experiences, require specific knowledge, experience, and expertise to conduct properly. Some, including those that use certain assessment instruments such as the Myers-Briggs Type Indicator (MBTI), require that trainers be certified. Think about whether qualified trainers will be available for the activities you would like to use. If not, look for alternatives.

Learning Preferences—The VAK Model

An important reason to vary the types of activities that you use to teach content is that different people have different preferences for the ways in which they like to learn. Some research suggests that there are three primary learning preferences—visual, auditory, and kinesthetic— based on the way we like to receive and process information. The VAK model, as it is commonly known, can be useful when you are thinking about what types of activities to meet your learners' differing needs. Here's an overview:

Visual learners may learn best when information is presented through pictures, diagrams, demonstrations, and other visual media or through reading and writing. Visual examples and illustrations such as slides, posters, flip charts, and props help them follow and understand what they hear, and taking notes helps them fix what they hear in their minds. More than half of the population may be primarily visual learners.

Auditory learners prefer to take in information through the ears and tend to remember more of what they hear than what they see. They learn well by listening and by talking. In training sessions, they prefer activities that involve listening and talking, such as lectures, brainstorming, and discussions. Some estimates are that 30 percent of people are primarily auditory learners.

Kinesthetic learners prefer doing to listening, talking, or observing. They like to take notes, draw pictures, or simply doodle when they are asked to listen, and they may lose focus when they need to sit still for too long. They do best with activities that let them move around and that provide hands-on practice. Far fewer people seem to be primary kinesthetic learners—perhaps less than 10 percent of the population.

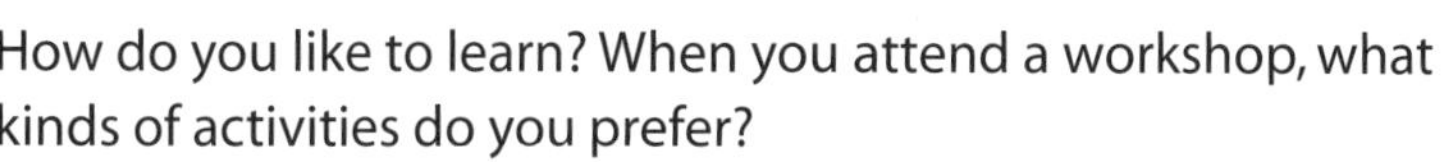

THINK ABOUT IT

How do you like to learn? When you attend a workshop, what kinds of activities do you prefer?

- *Learners' Characteristics*. Some people are likely to feel more comfortable with and learn more from certain kinds of activities than others. Some learn more easily when information is presented visually, some by listening, and some by talking and moving. Some are comfortable working in groups, others prefer to work alone. Learners who work in a collaborative, team-based environment may be more likely to enjoy and participate actively in collaborative learning experiences; those who are uncomfortable taking risks might not learn well from activities such as role plays in which they might make mistakes in front of others. If some learners have far less knowledge, skills, and/or experience than others, they may be unable or reluctant to participate in some kinds of activities or get much out of them if they do.

Consider Diverse Needs and Cultural Characteristics

There is no such thing as a "typical" learner in today's rapidly changing global workforce. When designing and selecting training activities, consider the learners with special needs; the characteristics and preferences of different generations; and the preferences of people from different cultures.

Vary the activities and the ways in which the trainer presents information so the training program will meet the needs of people with differing learning styles and preferences. Use visuals to support information that is presented verbally. Provide opportunities for individual reflection as well as group discussion. Create a learning environment in which people feel safe taking risks before asking them to do activities that they might consider risky. Use activities that get people on their feet and moving around once in a while. Allow people to opt-out of activities that make them feel uncomfortable.

- *Group size*. When planning activities, it's important to think about how many people will be attending the workshop. Some activities, such as round-table discussions and certain games, require a minimum number of people to be effective, while others, such as delivering practice presentations, work best in smaller groups.

To Consider When Selecting Activities

- The purpose of the activity.
- Available resources and time
- Relevance
- Qualifications of instructor
- The type of learning
- Group size
- Level of engagement
- Timing and pacing

- *Level of engagement*. The most useful activities are those that capture the learners' attention and are challenging enough to hold their interest. If learners can have fun, that's fine—but keep in mind that fun should be only a by-product, not the goal.
- *Timing*. Activities that work well in the morning may not work nearly so well at three o'clock in the afternoon when people are tired and thinking about what they're going to have for dinner. Conversely, once a workshop is well underway, learners might be willing to take a risk that would have made them uncomfortable at the beginning.

Think about the times of day when learners' energy is likely to be high, and when it is likely to be low. Generally, people have more energy and are able to concentrate better in the morning; in the post-lunch period, quiet, reflective activities might put some people to sleep. Consider the overall pacing—repeating the same kind of activity over and over can lend a monotonous rhythm to the workshop and fail to provide enough variety to meet different learning styles.

2. Components of an Experiential Learning Activity

Check What You Know

Which statements about experiential learning activities are accurate?

1. ____ Whenever trainers introduce an activity, they should carefully explain what the participants can expect to learn.
2. ____ If participants get stuck during the activity, trainers should help them discover the solution on their own instead of telling them how to solve the problem.
3. ____ The purpose of the debriefing, or processing, component of the activity is for the trainer to summarize his or her observations of what went on.
4. ____ At the end of the activity, learners should have an opportunity to apply or think about how they can apply what they have learned.

Your participants' brains are your best allies. . . . The brain doesn't just receive information—it processes it. Our job, as trainers, is to facilitate that processing.

Mel Silberman,
Training the Active Way

In *Creative Training Techniques*, Bob Pike describes a simple application of adult learning theory to the structure of group involvement activities that he calls the Activity/Discussion/Application (ADA) approach:

1. Do an activity.
2. Discuss what went on.
3. Consider how what went on applies to the real world.

Discovery Learning

The principles of "discovery learning" are attributed to psychologist Jerome Bruner, although his theories were based on the work of earlier researchers into the learning process, including Jean Piaget and John Dewey. Bruner postulated that people learn best through active engagement, drawing on their existing knowledge and experience to discover facts and relationships for themselves. The theory is not without controversy—some critics believe that learners need a certain amount of experience and prior knowledge for discovery learning to be effective. But this approach does seem to promote the engagement and interaction that are essential for learning.

For me, the word that best describes this approach is "discovery," because instead of being told something, learners discover it on their own, by doing the activity. They draw on their own experiences and knowledge and relate what they learn to their real worlds—key principles of adult learning.

Bob Pike's ADA model is a variation of the experiential learning model that guides the design of successful learning activities. Not all activities in a training program follow the experiential learning model, but the ones that do share common characteristics: they have, at a minimum, an introduction that prepares learners for the activity; the activity itself; a "debriefing" that helps learners process what they have learned; and an opportunity to apply or think about how to apply the learning.

Let's look more closely at each of those components.

The Introduction

The trainer tells learners what they are going to do and provides any instructions they need. Depending on the nature and purpose of the activity, the introduction might include a *brief* explanation of a theory or concept or a demonstration that learners need before engaging in the experience. Although some activities require detailed instructions, many require very little introduction and little setup. Sometimes only a few words of introduction are needed: "Now let's do an activity to try out some of these techniques."

To plan an introduction, think about what participants need to—and should—know before they begin. Remember that the purpose is for learners to discover something on their own, so the trainer should avoid telling them what they are supposed to learn. If the activity is lengthy and complicated, with lots of steps, the trainer will need to give careful verbal instructions, provide the instructions on a slide or flip-chart page that remains visible as people work, and clarify to make sure learners have understood the instructions before they begin.

Setting Up an Activity

Some activities require time and effort for setup—distributing materials, rearranging the room, setting up props or equipment, even moving to another location. Here are suggestions to keep the setup from becoming cumbersome:

- Leave enough time in the agenda for setup tasks so that the learners do not need to rush through any part of the activity.
- Plan for the setup in the sequence of the activities—if possible, schedule the activity after a break or lunch so that the setup can be done while participants are out of the room.
- If participants need to be present while the activity is being set up, determine how they can be involved in the process so they don't just sit around and wait.

The Activity

Participants engage in the activity while the trainer monitors their work to make sure they are on track and to answer questions if they get stuck. The trainer should be careful to remain in the background, not to join in as a participant, and not to jump in too quickly if people seem to be having trouble. A certain amount of stumbling is part of the learning process.

The trainer can offer help if the participants seem to be stuck or are seriously off track. But instead of telling people how to solve the problem, the trainer should help them discover the solution on their own by saying things like, "What's going on right now?" and "Why do you think you are having trouble with . . . ?

The Debriefing (Processing What Happened)

When the activity is over, learners need time and guidance to make sense of what they have experienced, done, or observed, and to connect the learning to their own experiences. This is an essential part of the experience; without it, the activity may have little or no meaning and provide little or no learning.

To debrief the activity, provide questions such as those below that help learners think about, reflect on, and perhaps discuss what happened:

- "What was that activity like for you?"
- "What did you observe?"
- "What happened?"
- "What common themes or general principles did you notice?"
- "What did you learn about yourself/the process?"
- "What are the implications of what you learned?"
- "In what ways does this experience relate to your real world?"
- "Has this experience changed the way you see [or understand] . . . ?

Learners can answer these questions individually, but it is usually more useful if they discuss the questions with others—with another participant, in small groups, or with the whole group—so they can learn from other people's ideas and points of view.

Application of the Learning

Keep in mind that the goal of training is to effect change. The purpose of this component is to help learners connect what they have learned to their real world and change the way they do things. To help them make that connection and think about change, you can provide such questions as:

- "What do the results of this activity have to do with your real world?"
- "What can/will you do to use what you've learned?"
- "What changes will you make in the way you do XYZ?"
- "What will you do differently as a result of this experience?"

Participants can answer these questions on their own or discuss them with others. As you'll see later in this chapter, they can also make action plans that spell out specific steps they will take to apply the learning.

What/So What/Now What?

The experiential learning approach guides learners through the process of answering three important questions: "What?" "So What?" "Now What?"

"WHAT . . . happened during this activity? What did you feel? What did you notice?" For example, learners in a team-building workshop who have worked together to come up with the solution to a problem might say, "I noticed that we jumped right to brainstorming possible solutions, without ever discussing the root causes of the problem" or "I felt as if we stopped listening to one another halfway through the process."

"SO WHAT . . . did you learn from this experience? In what ways did the experience help you understand/change your perceptions of thus and so? What conclusions can you draw? What are the implications?" Learners in the team-building workshop might say, "I learned that one reason we have trouble coming up with workable solutions to problems is that we seldom bother to identify the root causes—we're addressing the symptoms, not the problems" or "When we don't listen to one another, we miss or ignore important information and ideas." They might also say, "We waste a lot of time because we're not paying enough attention to the process and to one another—and we waste more time dealing with problems we should have solved at earlier stages."

"NOW WHAT . . . can you do with this learning? How can you apply what you've learned? How will what you learned be useful?" In the team-building workshop, learners might say, "We will pay more attention to the way we solve problems—follow the steps in the process more carefully—make sure that we know that we're addressing the real problem before we come up with a solution and take the time to listen to one another's ideas."

3. Types of Activities

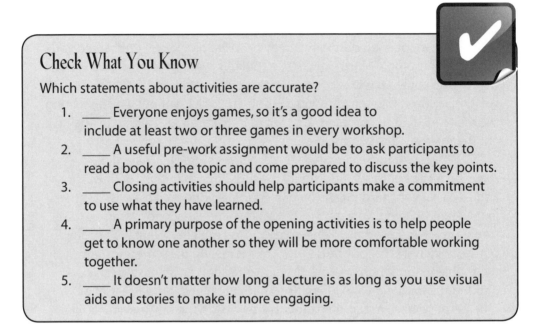

Check What You Know

Which statements about activities are accurate?

1. ____ Everyone enjoys games, so it's a good idea to include at least two or three games in every workshop.
2. ____ A useful pre-work assignment would be to ask participants to read a book on the topic and come prepared to discuss the key points.
3. ____ Closing activities should help participants make a commitment to use what they have learned.
4. ____ A primary purpose of the opening activities is to help people get to know one another so they will be more comfortable working together.
5. ____ It doesn't matter how long a lecture is as long as you use visual aids and stories to make it more engaging.

As Boris and Marietta discovered, the sheer number of possible activities can make the selection process daunting. When sorting through the options to decide what activities to use in the various segments of a training program, it can help to know something about the general categories into which they fall.

Pre-Work

Assignments that learners complete before the training program begins help to prepare them for training and save time during training. For example, when I conducted business writing workshops, I asked participants to complete a questionnaire and a brief writing assignment and send them to me a week before the workshop. Completing the questionnaire started people thinking about their expectations for the workshop and how what they were going to learn related to their work; their responses and writing samples helped me tailor the workshop to their needs.

Examples of pre-work activities include:

- Something to read, such as a case study that will be discussed in the workshop
- A video or podcast that provides background information about or an introduction to the topic
- A questionnaire that elicits information about participants' expectations for and concerns about the training program
- An assessment instrument that participants will debrief during the workshop
- A project or research assignment that engages participants with the subject in advance

When using pre-work, it's very important to remember that the workshop is only one event on the learners' overcrowded calendars. Keep pre-work assignments brief and relevant. Explain clearly what learners are expected to do, how the pre-work will be used in the workshop, and how doing the pre-work will benefit them. Asking people to submit something by a specific date—a completed assessment or questionnaire, answers to questions about a case study or a podcast—and following up with those who do not makes it more likely that everyone will actually do the pre-work.

Opening Activities

The activities used to open a workshop are among the few that may not be directly related to a specific learning objective, but they are very important nonetheless. It's during the opening that the trainer establishes rapport with participants, helps them get to know one another and feel comfortable in the training environment, sets the tone for the workshop, stimulates people's interest in the topic, engages participants in the learning process, and helps people see how the workshop will benefit them. Relevant opening activities set a workshop up for success.

Here are some of the things that opening activities should accomplish:

- Help people get to know one another. When you arrive at a party that's filled with strangers, the sooner you get to know some of the other guests, the sooner you are likely to feel comfortable so you can have a good time. Workshop experiences are similar. Unless the workshop is to

About Icebreakers

In *Training the Active Way*, Mel Silberman describes two types of icebreakers: social icebreakers and learning icebreakers. Both types are ways of involving people immediately and helping them feel comfortable in the training environment. The key difference is that social icebreakers focus on helping people get to know one another, while learning icebreakers focus on the subject of the training program.

There's no need to choose one over the other. Some social icebreakers are also learning icebreakers, and vice versa. I've found that the best icebreakers accomplish several purposes: they kick off the workshop on a lively note, encourage people to participate immediately, help people establish rapport and feel comfortable in the training environment—and are relevant to the content.

be delivered to members of a team who work closely together, chances are that participants will not know everyone in the room, and it is often the case that the participants are strangers to one another. The sooner that people get to know one another, the more comfortable they will be; the more comfortable they are, the easier it will be for them to learn.

- Engage participants in the learning process. People often come to a workshop expecting to sit passively while a trainer lectures and shows videos. Opening activities that start people talking, moving, and sharing ideas and information send the message that this will be a learner-centered, not a trainer-centered, workshop in which participants will learn through active participation.
- Help learners think about what they want to accomplish and how the training will benefit them. People arrive at a workshop with one overriding question: What's in it for me? They want to know what they are going to accomplish and how what they learn will help them achieve their goals more easily, more quickly, and more successfully. Opening activities that accomplish those purposes go a long way toward engaging people and getting them ready to learn.

You want participants to remember what they've learned. You also want participants to feel that what they learned has been special.

Mel Silberman,
Training the Active Way

Closing Activities

Just as opening activities prepare learners for the work that is to come, closing activities help them remember what they've learned and transfer the learning to the workplace. Like opening activities, most closing activities are not directly related to specific learning objectives, but to the goals of the program as a whole. They should accomplish the following:

- Reinforce the key learning points by providing an opportunity for learners to review what they've learned
- Give participants a chance to think about what they have learned and how it relates to their goals
- Help learners decide on next steps and make a commitment to use what they have learned
- Give learners a chance to ask questions
- Help learners identify ways in which they can continue learning
- Provide learners with a sense of closure and accomplishment

Interactive Lectures

As we've discussed earlier, experts in adult learning agree that people do not generally learn well by passively receiving information—in other words, by sitting and listening to a lecture. Yet every training program includes some content—perhaps a lot of content—that needs to be delivered from the trainer to the participants. When you can't find a practical alternative, look for ways to make lectures more interesting and more interactive, so that learners remain engaged and involved. Here are some suggestions:

- Intersperse questions such as, "Who can give us an examples of . . . ?" "Can someone tell us about an experience with . . . ?" "What would be a good way of . . . ?" "Can anyone explain how to . . . ?" Make sure that

Action Planning

It's a fact that we're all much better at doing what we say we're going to do if we identify concrete actions that we will take and give ourselves deadlines. Workshop participants who make action plans are much more likely to go beyond, "I'm going to do a much better job of planning meetings" (or giving feedback, writing reports, solving problems, or anything else) and make real, meaningful changes in their behavior or performance.

To be useful, action plans should be:

- *Limited in scope.* One reason that people don't do what they say they are going to do is that they have taken on too much. An action plan should address only one or two goals at a time.
- *Lay out concrete steps.* Vague actions are likely to have vague results. An action plan should describe specific actions for achieving the goal.
- *Specify when the actions will be taken.* Action plans should include the time frame within which the actions will be taken or the deadline by which the goal will be achieved.
- *If appropriate, specify necessary resources and assistance.* People often need help if they are going to make changes. An action plan should identify money, time, equipment, materials, help from others, and other resources that are essential for achieving the goal, and describe how those resources will be obtained.
- *Be shared with someone else.* We are all more likely to do what we say we're going to do when we've made our commitment public in some way. Sharing an action plan verbally or in writing with colleagues and/or managers helps firm up that commitment.

every question helps learners interact with the content in some way. A question such as, "Does everyone understand?" or "Does anyone have any questions?" doesn't make a lecture interactive. Instead, design questions so that they help learners think about the content and connect it with their own experiences and knowledge.

- Writing things down helps many people stay attentive and get more out of the content during a lecture. Note-taking pages with prompts that encourage learners to write down key points and ideas can be very helpful.
- Keep the uninterrupted portions of lectures short. Break the content up into chunks so that the trainer does not speak for more than about ten minutes without asking questions or giving participants another activity. Use stories and visuals to illustrate abstract concepts.

> *Lively, focused discussions are often the best moments in a training session. Participants are engaged, and time flies.*
>
> Mel Silberman,
> *Training the Active Way*

Group Discussions and Projects

This category covers a broad range of activities that are designed to promote learning. The trainer might pose a problem, hand out a set of questions, or assign a task; learners work together to analyze the problem, answer the questions, or do the task. They then present or summarize their work for their colleagues, reflect on the experience, draw out the key learning points, and explore ways in which they can use what they have learned.

Like other activities, discussions and projects work best when they are carefully planned so that the questions and assignments guide participants toward the discovery of key learning points. The instructions have to be clear enough so that

The Value of Stories

When you design a training program, include stories, give trainers guidelines for selecting their own, and suggest that the trainer encourage participants to share their own stories. Not only do people enjoy listening to stories, but relevant stories liven up a training presentation and increase the learners' understanding. Stories help people visualize ideas and concepts and make connections between their own experiences and what they are learning, and they are excellent ways to kick off discussions and collaborative activities.

participants know exactly what they are expected to do, without "giving away" the learning points. As mentioned earlier, while giving groups enough leeway to stumble a little, trainers need to stand by to answer questions and step in to help if a group goes too far off track or becomes too stuck.

Case Studies

A case study is a scenario or description of a real or realistic situation. Learners work together or on their own to discover key learning points from the case, apply what they are learning to the case, or examine how the case exemplifies what they are learning. A relevant, well-written case study engages and involves learners, increasing the chances that they will be able to remember and apply what they learn.

Case studies can be very simple or very complex—and anywhere in between. You can develop your own or purchase prepared cases. Even better, participants can develop their own case studies, based on real or realistic job-related situations.

When developing or selecting cases, consider including the following:

- The content of the case must be realistic, relevant to the learning objectives, and something to which learners can relate.
- The case must be complex and challenging enough so that learners cannot come up with a quick, easy, black-and-white assessment and conclusion, but not so difficult that they become frustrated.
- There must be enough time for learners to read and analyze the case, discover or apply the key learning points, and reflect on what they have learned.

Demonstrations

People don't learn by watching; they learn by doing. But when combined with opportunities for practice, a demonstration that shows how something is done or that models behavior can be an effective instructional strategy. For example, learners can watch the trainer or someone else set up a piece of equipment and then try it themselves. They can view a video showing a job interview, analyze what they saw, come up with some interview guidelines and strategies, and then do a role play to practice what they have learned.

Traditionally, the person doing the demonstration explains the process or the procedure while showing how it works. But in *Training the Active Way*, author Mel Silberman suggests that trainers omit the explanation. "Instead of telling participants what you are doing," he advises, "[ask them] to observe carefully the demonstration and tell you what you did. This strategy encourages participants to be mentally alert." For example, the trainer might show a video clip of a manager giving feedback to an employee about a task the employee has just completed; ask participants what they observed; then ask participants to try it themselves by giving feedback to one another in a simulated situation.

Learner-Generated Cases

Instead of analyzing a prepared case, learners can develop their own, which has the benefit of helping them draw on their own experiences and relate the analysis more easily to their real world. For example, in a workshop on delegating, one of the people in a small group can describe work that he or she needs to delegate and the characteristics (not the name) of the employee to whom the work will be delegated. Once the case has been developed, the group members can come up with strategies for delegating that work. In a workshop on marketing, a small group could build a case based on a real situation in which marketing efforts are not working, analyze the situation, and come up with some solutions.

Practice Exercises

One edition of the Webster's *New Collegiate Dictionary* defines practice as "to perform or work at repeatedly so as to become proficient." Practice is essential for learning a skill, whether it's driving a car, changing a tire, serving a tennis ball, baking a cake, creating a spreadsheet, negotiating a deal, writing a report, making a presentation, or interviewing candidates for a job. Practice exercises let learners try out new skills, strategies, and techniques in a safe situation in which they can receive feedback from the trainer and others and learn from mistakes.

But how much practice should be included in a given workshop? There are no easy answers to that question. One consideration is how difficult the task is to do and how important it is that learners be able to do it right before trying it out on the job. For example, I would expect a surgeon to have a tremendous amount of practice in simulated situations before performing her first operation. Another thing to consider is whether people will have sufficient opportunities to practice what they learn on the job as soon as training is

Guidelines for Giving Feedback

Feedback is an important part of the learning process. But trainers and participants often do not know how to give useful feedback, so it helps to provide some guidelines in the training materials. For example:

- Feedback should always focus on the behavior, not the person. Instead of, "You were rude to the customer during the role play," say, "You did not smile at the customer."
- Be specific—say what you observed, without comments. Instead of, "I didn't think you were very professional during that presentation," say, "You stood in a slumped body position and spoke too quickly."

If giving feedback will be very important during the training program, consider including a checklist that the trainer and/or the participants can use to give feedback on specific aspects of a learner's behavior.

completed. If they might not use what they learn often or right away, they may need more practice during training.

Games

Games can be a great alternative to lecture when people need to acquire knowledge such as facts and statistics or review key learning points. Games can add variety to a training program and engage people in material that might otherwise be somewhat dry.

Entire books are devoted to games that you can use or adapt for training; you can also develop your own. A board game based on Monopoly or Risk can help learners apply and practice concepts, principles, or strategies. Puzzles can provide problem-solving challenges. Games like Concentration or Trivial Pursuit can help learners memorize or classify facts.

Like other activities, games should never appear trivial or meaningless. They should always have a specific purpose and be clearly linked to the learning objectives. Also, while most people enjoy games, some do not, so it's important to have a good understanding of the audience when deciding whether to use games and what games to use.

Role Plays

Role plays, in which two or more people act out a scenario and receive feedback from the trainer and/or their colleagues, can be used for demonstration, discovery, and practice. Trainers might ask for volunteers to role play a negotiation, ask participants what they observed, and lead a discussion about negotiation strategies. Learners might use role plays to practice giving performance feedback, reflect on and discuss the experience, and then try it again. Sales representatives can use role plays to practice closing a sale.

Keep in mind that role playing falls into the "risky" category for many people. Role-play activities should be used only after there has been sufficient opportunity for learners to establish trust. Even then, trainers should never force people to get up and "act" in front of their colleagues. A less risky way to gain the benefits of role play is for people to do the activity in pairs or groups of three, instead of in front of the entire group.

Simulations

Simulations give learners the chance to practice skills, carry out procedures, and make decisions in a safe training environment that has as many of the characteristics of the real world as possible. As mentioned above, a surgeon-in-training might use simulations to try out surgical techniques before operating on a person. Airline pilots routinely practice with simulations before getting behind the controls of a real plane. A team might engage in a simulation that helps them learn about cooperation, negotiation, collaboration, and risk-assessment. Managers might use a complex scenario to develop a strategic plan for a fictitious company or discover ways to turn around a dysfunctional organization. A group of marketing specialists might develop marketing plans for a fictitious business. Well-designed simulations can be very useful ways to help people learn and practice complex thinking, analysis, problem solving, and interactive skills.

Gaming technology has made it possible to develop simulations that are based on incredibly realistic worlds in which learners can meet and interact. Those kinds of simulations are ideal for people to learn in situations such as fighting fires or preparing for combat operations in which the real environment would be dangerous. The realistic nature of a good simulation can provide an extremely engaging and powerful learning experience in other situations as well.

Good simulations take time to develop and time to conduct. There are some excellent off-the-shelf simulations available or, if you have the time and expertise, you can develop your own.

Reflection

Group discussions, practice exercises, games, role plays, and other activities that learners do together keep a workshop lively and engaging. But learners also need opportunities to pause from time to time to examine their observations and feelings, relate the learning to their own experiences, and consider what kinds of changes they might want to make in their behavior. Reflective activities are like stopping by the side of the road on a trip to think about where you've been and where you're going. Although they take many forms, the most common is for learners to answer questions about what they have been learning and what it means to them. The trainer might invite them to share their responses with the group or with partners, but they should always be allowed to keep their responses private.

Application

In the end, the best way to cement learning is to apply it. Application activities let learners try out the learning in a real—not simulated—situation. A team can work together to come up with solutions to a real, current problem. Mechanics can repair a real engine. Marketing professionals can design a real marketing campaign. Managers can write real quarterly performance reports. Learners might stumble at first. They might need to repeat the activity more than once. They need a chance to reflect on the experience and receive feedback on their performance. But application activities are the purest form of learning by doing—which is, as we know, the way adults learn best.

Types of Learning Activities

Type of Activity	Used to . . .	What to Consider
Lecture: A one-way communication in which the trainer delivers information to learners	Get facts and concepts across in a relatively short amount of time when interactivity is not needed	Learners are passive, not active; keep lectures brief and use them sparingly; use stories, concrete examples, visuals, and props to engage learners; follow lectures with an activity in which learners interact with the instructor and/or one another or use the information in some way
Interactive lecture: A lecture with interactive elements such as questions and discussions	Make lectures more engaging by providing opportunities for learners to interact with the material	Limit lecture "chunks" (when trainer is speaking) to five or ten minutes, with interactive element between chunks
Structured discussions: Learners discuss a topic, usually in small groups, and summarize their discussion for the larger group	Help learners examine, analyze, and explore a topic; express ideas and share opinions; share their knowledge and experience; work together to solve problems	Helps participants relate what they are learning to what they already know; highly engaging and interactive; can be time-consuming; may need careful facilitation to help groups stay on topic
Observations and demonstrations: Learners watch the trainer, other learners, or someone else do something	Show learners how to do a task, carry out a process, behave in a certain way, interact with others	Usually capture learners' interest; must be accurate, slow, and clearly presented enough for people to follow, and accompanied by necessary explanations; works best when immediately followed by opportunity to practice
Role plays: Learners follow a script or instructions to act out a real or realistic situation	Help learners practice and experiment with new techniques; can provide insights into their own and other people's behaviors	Involve learners and help them learn by doing; take careful planning; can be time-consuming; some learners find role plays uncomfortable; work best when learners give and receive feedback and have a chance to reflect on their experiences

(*Continued*)

Type of Activity	Used to ...	What to Consider
Case studies: Learners read, analyze, and discuss a written description of a situation, usually a problem or the way someone solved a problem	Help learners apply what they are learning and learn by discovery; encourage collaboration and help learners draw on what they already know to identify and solve problems	Engaging and interactive; most learners find relevant, well-written cases engaging and interesting, although some want to be given a black-and-white resolution; cases can be difficult to write, and the activity can take a lot of time
Questionnaires and assessments: Learners answer questions or complete a rating instrument that helps them evaluate their knowledge, skill level, attitudes, and feelings; may include comparison with observers' responses to same questions	Help learners understand and reflect on their personal relationships to what they are learning and determine what they may need to improve or change	Most learners like to complete these types of assessments, although some find them uncomfortable; questions need to be carefully designed and accompanied by careful facilitation to be relevant and useful; learners need to do something with the feedback
Games: Learners compete with one another (or with themselves) to answer questions or perform tasks; involve rules and may include rewards for winners	Help learners learn facts, practice tasks, solve problems, come up with new ideas, review and reinforce what they have learned	Fun, engaging way of learning that can be done in a group or individually (learners play against themselves); game must be carefully designed to achieve a specific purpose; some learners find games "silly"
Practice exercises: Learners practice doing what they have learned and receive feedback	Help learners learn by doing—try out new learning, experiment, and make adjustments	Engaging; can be done individually or with others; helps learners prepare to apply learning to the real world
Simulations: Activities that attempt to provide a realistic real-world experience	Helps learners apply the learning in a situation that closely approximates their real world	Can be very engaging and involving; can help learners transfer learning to their real world; can be costly and time-consuming to conduct

Boris and Marietta's Progress

Here are some of the activities that Boris and Marietta plan to use in the e-mail workshop:

- A learning icebreaker in which participants introduce themselves to someone they don't know and share a story about e-mail they have sent or received
- A small-group discussion in which participants come up with the criteria for a useful e-mail message by discussing a poorly written e-mail with inappropriate content, identifying possible consequences of the e-mail, and deciding what advice they would give the writer
- A small-group project in which participants work together to plan an e-mail message in a given situation
- An individual application exercise in which participants apply what they are learning by critiquing and revising an e-mail message of their own
- A large group activity in which participants write guidelines for using e-mail productively

Quick Quiz

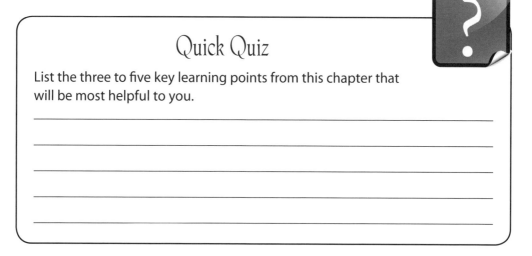

List the three to five key learning points from this chapter that will be most helpful to you.

____

____

____

____

____

What's Next?

Once you've identified the content and learning activities for the training program, you're ready to pull everything together—to decide on the sequence of objectives, topics, and activities; design an opening and closing; check the timing; prepare an agenda; and identify the materials that the program requires. That's what you'll learn about in the next chapter.

Apply What You Learn

Describe some of the learning activities you will use in your training program. Include the purpose of each activity.

Learning Objective: ______________________________

Activity:	Purpose:
______________________	______________________
______________________	______________________
______________________	______________________
Activity:	Purpose:
______________________	______________________
______________________	______________________
______________________	______________________
Activity:	Purpose:
______________________	______________________
______________________	______________________
______________________	______________________

Learning Objective: ______________________________

Activity:	Purpose:
Activity:	Purpose:
Activity:	Purpose:

Learning Objective: ______________________________

Activity:	Purpose:
Activity:	Purpose:
Activity:	Purpose:

(Continued)

Learning Objective: ____

Activity:	Purpose:
______________________	______________________
______________________	______________________
Activity:	Purpose:
______________________	______________________
______________________	______________________
Activity:	Purpose:
______________________	______________________
______________________	______________________

Learning Objective: ____

Activity:	Purpose:
______________________	______________________
______________________	______________________
Activity:	Purpose:
______________________	______________________
______________________	______________________
Activity:	Purpose:
______________________	______________________
______________________	______________________

Answers to Exercises

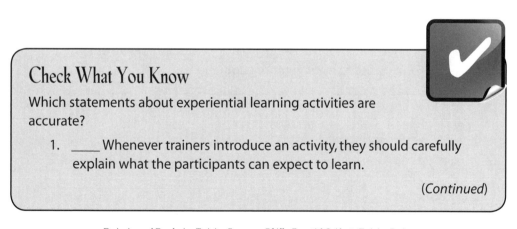

Check What You Know

For a team workshop on problem solving, one of the learning objectives is to "Identify the root causes of a problem in a given situation." Which of the scenarios below describes an activity that is most likely to help people achieve that objective? Why?

1. _X_ The trainer elicits a list of current problems from the group, asks people to work in small groups to come up with possible root causes, and then asks each group to summarize its process.
2. ___ The trainer shows several slides describing situations in which there is a problem. For each situation, the trainer asks learners to choose a possible root cause from a list. She tallies the responses.

The first activity would be more likely to engage learners, be more relevant, stimulate their thinking, help them relate what they are learning to what they already know, help them learn through discovery and from one another, give them a chance to practice, and help them transfer the learning to their real world.

Check What You Know

Which statements about experiential learning activities are accurate?

1. ____ Whenever trainers introduce an activity, they should carefully explain what the participants can expect to learn.

(*Continued*)

2. _X_ If participants get stuck during the activity, trainers should help them discover the solution on their own instead of telling them how to solve the problem.
3. ___ The purpose of the debriefing, or processing, component of the activity is for the trainer to summarize his or her observations of what went on.
4. _X_ At the end of the activity, learners should have an opportunity to apply or think about how they can apply what they have learned.

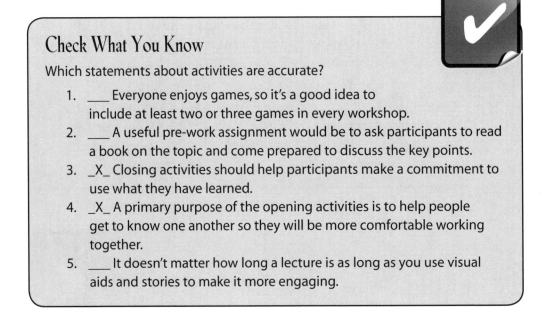

Check What You Know

Which statements about activities are accurate?

1. ___ Everyone enjoys games, so it's a good idea to include at least two or three games in every workshop.
2. ___ A useful pre-work assignment would be to ask participants to read a book on the topic and come prepared to discuss the key points.
3. _X_ Closing activities should help participants make a commitment to use what they have learned.
4. _X_ A primary purpose of the opening activities is to help people get to know one another so they will be more comfortable working together.
5. ___ It doesn't matter how long a lecture is as long as you use visual aids and stories to make it more engaging.

7

Structuring a Training Program

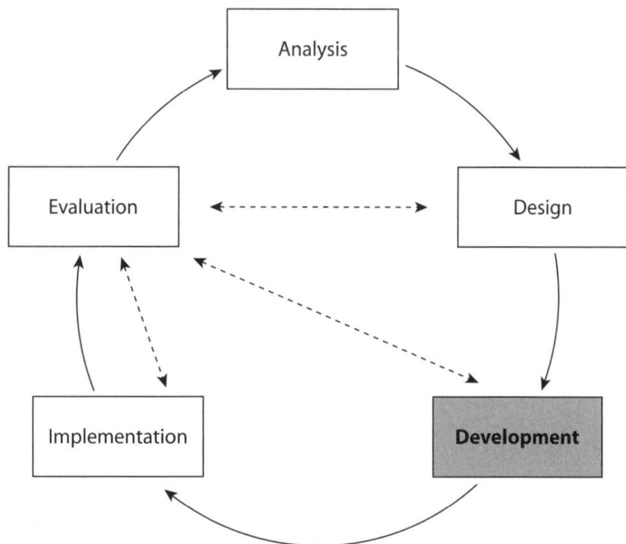

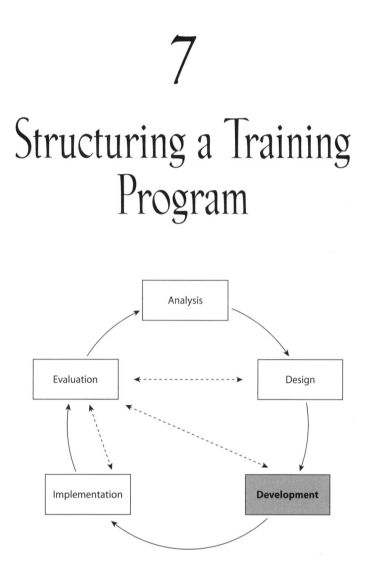

The Development Stage of the ADDIE Model

Check What You Know

Boris and Marietta had just started working on the training program one morning when the HR director stopped by. "How's everything going?" he asked.

"Fine," they said, almost in unison.

"I'd like to tell the CEO when we'll have an agenda and a time frame," the HR director said.

Boris and Marietta looked at one another. "By the end of this week?" Marietta suggested?

"Sure," Boris said.

"Great," the HR director said. "I'll tell her."

After the HR director left, Boris turned to Marietta. "Okay, let's go over what we need to do."

"I think this is the place where we put all the pieces together," Marietta said. "An agenda—that's really just an outline of the content and the activities."

"And the timing, right?" Boris said.

Marietta nodded. "We need to figure out what visuals and media to use..."

"...and what materials we need to prepare," Boris added.

Boris and Marietta gathered up their laptops and their folders of notes and headed for a conference room, where they spent the rest of the morning outlining the structure of the workshop and figuring out what materials they'd need.

How do you think Boris and Marietta went about developing the structure of their training program?

____

____

____

____

When our children were young, my husband and I would often spend hours the night before their birthdays putting together a special toy like a bicycle or a playhouse. We would open the box (not always an easy thing to do) and dump the components out onto the floor. Then we'd study the instructions (usually written in some kind of code), trying to figure out how to put the thing together so that it resembled the picture on the box. Even though we knew where we were going—we had a picture, after all—we usually made many false starts, putting things together and taking them apart again several times before we got it right. Structuring a training program is like that. You have the components—the content and the activities. There's a good picture on the box—the desired outcome and the learning objectives. Now you need to assemble everything so that it works. That's what this chapter is about.

What's in this chapter:

- What's involved in structuring a training program
- The best sequence for the content and activities
- Planning the opening and closing
- Checking the timing
- Identifying the visuals, media, and training aids the program requires
- Preparing an agenda

There is something inherently fascinating about putting things together. . . . Drawing together all the disparate elements [of a training program] is a challenging, frustrating, yet . . . exhilarating experience.

Harold D. Stolovitch, "Front-End Analysis, Implementation Planning, and Evaluation," in T.L. Gargiulo, A.M. Pangarkar, and T. Kirkwood (Eds.), *The Trainer's Portable Mentor*

1. What's Involved in Structuring a Training Program

By the time you've reach this phase of the instructional design process, you've done most of the hard work. You have all the pieces, you probably have a good idea of how the program will be structured, and you are likely to have a preliminary agenda or outline. Now it's time to pull everything together into a sequence of content and activities that flow logically and provide a cohesive experience that helps people learn.

Although this chapter focuses on structuring a workshop, many of the tasks, such as determining the sequence of content and activities, are the same for other types of programs. Those tasks usually include the following:

- Determining the sequence of topics and activities
- Planning the opening and closing
- Checking the timing
- Identifying the visuals, media, and training aids for each point in the program
- Preparing a detailed agenda that includes estimated times for each program segment
- Identifying the materials that need to be developed or obtained

2. Determining the Sequence

Just as every trip has a beginning and an end, every workshop has an opening and a closing. The challenge is figuring out the best sequence for everything that comes in between. It's like putting together a puzzle: you might need to arrange and rearrange the components until you discover how they fit together.

In many cases, the objectives suggest a logical sequence. For example, for novice cooks to be able to follow a recipe to make an apple pie, they would first need to understand abbreviations such as "tsp" and know how to carry out procedures such as "roll out the dough." To practice conducting a job interview, managers first need to recognize questions that cannot legally be asked of job applicants and be able to distinguish between closed-ended and open-ended questions.

No matter what methodology you use, what's important is to find a sequence of topics and activities that fosters learning. Here's a process you can use if a logical sequence doesn't quickly become clear.

1. Write each component—each objective, each activity, each topic—on an index card or a Post-it Note, or enter them into a software program that will allow you to move items around easily. Arrange and rearrange the components into groupings of items that seem to belong together. If a topic or activity doesn't seem to belong with any of the objectives, set it aside.

Sequencing Schemes

Here are the typical ways of sequencing the content and activities in a training program:

- Priority—Arrange topics in order of what people need to know first, second, and so on.
- Familiar to unfamiliar—Present material that is familiar to learners before presenting new concepts and techniques.
- Easy to challenging—Organize the material so that people learn the easier concepts, skills, and techniques first, then progress to those that are more difficult.
- Logical progression—Arrange the topics in an order that seems to make the most sense.
- General to specific—Present general concepts and principles or procedural overviews first, then drill down into the details.
- Comfortable to risky—Organize the material so that riskier activities come after people have had a chance to feel safe in the learning environment.
- Simple to complex—Arrange concepts, skills, and techniques in order of complexity.

2. Keep moving things around until a logical order emerges. If none does, or if some of the components seem especially reluctant to fit in anywhere, take a break and then give it another try. You might find that you don't really need that component.
3. If the right sequence still does not become clear, stop and take a step back. Are you sure that the learning objectives clearly describe what people need to do when this program is completed? Are there any learning objectives that need to be revised? Eliminated? Added? Are you sure that each topic and activity has a clear purpose and is clearly linked to an objective?

Chances are that by this time in the process, you will not have to go back and redo key elements of the design, although you might have to eliminate or replace some of the topics and activities. But if the design seems to be faulty, go back to the beginning and rethink everything. It's better to do that now, before starting the time-consuming task of developing the program materials.

To Consider When Developing the Sequence

When you decide on the best sequence for the content and activities, think about what you've learned about how people stay engaged in training and how they learn. Here are some things to keep in mind:

- *People learn by building on what they already know.* Thus, it's usually best to present easier, more familiar concepts before moving on to more unfamiliar and more challenging concepts. There are exceptions, in which learners take a stab at the "big" concepts first, then break them down, but I've found that, with most groups, it's better to use what people are already familiar with or know as a springboard for helping them learn new skills and grasp new concepts.
- *It's worth repeating that people need to feel safe in the learning environment before they are able to take risks.* One reason that some people resist training is that they have had uncomfortable, sometimes embarrassing, experiences in training situations. Asking people to risk volunteering ideas or opinions, making mistakes, or appearing awkward or clumsy before they feel confident that the trainer and the other participants will be supportive can keep them from becoming engaged enough to learn.
- *Variety is the spice of life—and of training programs.* Variety in pacing, activities, and presentation methods helps keep people awake, interested, and attentive. Follow a long activity with a short one. Vary the way in which the trainer presents information. Intersperse activities in which people work on their own or with a partner with those in which they work in groups. Get people up on their feet and moving around once in a while.
- *For the program to flow seamlessly, with one segment moving effortlessly into the next, the order of content and activities needs to make sense.* To return to an example from an earlier chapter, before job-seekers can learn how to complete a job application, they need to know what an application is, how it is used, what kinds of information they'll be asked to provide, and where to find that information. Even in situations in which topics could be presented in no specific order, think about the order that is most likely to help people learn.

The Principle of Chunking

According to research by psychologist George A. Miller and others, people learn and remember information better when it is presented in manageable "chunks." The most common example is the telephone number. It's easier to remember a phone number that is broken up into chunks—415-792-6043—than one in which the numbers all run together: 4157926043.

The research found that that there is a limit on how much information people can grasp and retain at one time. For complex information that is new, there should be no more than seven "chunks"; for less complex information that is already familiar, a chunk can contain as many as nine items.

For those of us who design training, the point is that we need to break down information so that people can understand and retain what they learn: smaller chunks with less information when people are learning new topics and processes; larger chunks with more information for people who already know a lot about what they are learning.

3. Planning the Opening and the Closing

In Chapter 6, you learned about what the workshop opening and closing need to accomplish. Part of the process of developing the program sequence is to plan an opening that gets the workshop started smoothly and a closing that wraps everything up and sends participants on their way, ready to use what they have learned.

The Opening

You already know that the opening needs to stimulate the learners' interest, let them know how the workshop will benefit them, and

Using the Objectives to Determine the Sequence

1. List the learning objectives in a logical order (what do learners need to know first, second, etc.; the steps in a process; simple to complex; familiar to new).
2. For each learning objective, list the topics and activities in a logical order.

Using Activities to Determine Sequence

1. List the activities in a logical order (familiar to new; less risky to more risky; simple to complex; order of priority).
2. Indicate the objective that each activity will help learners achieve.
3. For each activity, describe the content learners need.

Using the Topics to Determine Sequence

1. List all the topics.
2. Group topics together.
3. List the key learning points for each topic.
4. List the activities for each key learning point.
5. Indicate the objective that each activity will help learners achieve.
6. Outline the content for each topic.

engage them actively. When you plan the opening, also decide how you will accomplish the following:

- *Give learners an overview of the workshop*. It's easier to reach a destination when you know how you will get there and can see the journey laid out on a map. The opening should provide participants with a road map of their journey—an overview of the sequence of content and activities.
- *Establish ground rules*. Ground rules, such as "cell phones off," "listen while others are speaking," and "come back on time from breaks," help a workshop run more smoothly. Participants are more likely to honor ground rules when they participate in establishing them, which can be done in a brief activity during the opening segment.
- *Provide logistical information*. The opening also needs to include a little business, such as the times for breaks and lunch, the location of restrooms, parking validations, and any other logistical information learners need. This information should be limited to what's important and be conveyed as quickly as possible. Leave a minute or so for logistics after the opening activities, just before the transition to the first segment of the workshop.

The Closing

As you learned in Chapter 6, the closing activities are very important to people's ability to use what they've learned. When you plan the opening:

- Include an activity that reinforces the key learning points.
- Provide an opportunity for learners to ask questions.
- Decide how to help learners make a commitment to action.
- Include a brief activity that helps people feel a sense of accomplishment for their hard work.
- Determine what else participants need to know or do before they leave (such as complete an evaluation form).

4. Checking the Timing

Check What You Know

Suppose you've been asked to design a one-day training program to provide product specialists with the skills for making presentations to management on new product ideas. One of the objectives is to be able to deliver a ten-minute presentation that meets specific standards. But for everyone in the group to practice delivering a presentation and obtain feedback, which you believe is an essential part of the learning process, the workshop would need to be extended to two days. What could you do?

____

____

____

____

Imagine attending a play in which the actors start to speed up their lines halfway through and then skip the scenes at the end. It would be a pretty unsatisfying experience. Unfortunately, that's what sometimes happens in a workshop. As the clock ticks, the trainer starts speaking more rapidly and truncating activities, or skipping them entirely. People are left wondering what's going on and unsure of what they were supposed to have learned.

Running out of time is one of a trainer's most common challenges. When trainers fall behind, they tend to cut discussions and activities short or convert them to lectures, eliminate breaks, and rush through the closing, if they get to it at all.

Inexperienced trainers often think that they run out of time because they've let people talk too much. I've rarely found that to be the case. Although trainers need to manage discussions to keep a workshop on track, running out of time usually means that the workshop design is unrealistic—there is simply too much content to cover, too many activities to do, and too many objectives to achieve in the given amount of time.

THINK ABOUT IT

Which strategy or strategies would be effective if you find that you have too much to cover in the time available for a one-day workshop that is scheduled to run from 8:30 to 4:30?

1. ____ Add time by starting the workshop at 7:30 and going until 5:30.
2. ____ Replace one or more time-consuming activities with activities that requires less time but are still effective ways of helping people achieve the learning objectives.
3. ____ Determine which learning objective requires the most time and eliminate it.
4. ____ Use another delivery method, such as e-learning, a webinar, or self-study, for some of the content.
5. ____ Determine whether some of the objectives could be split off into a separate training program.

People who have been designing training for a while understand how important time is to a successful workshop. They limit the number of learning objectives to those that can reasonably be achieved in the time available, even if that means developing two programs instead of one, and they think carefully about timing when selecting activities. They consider timing during the design process, so that when they reach the development stage, they have already made key decisions about what can be reasonably accomplished. Then, when they structure the program and develop the agenda, they take another very close look at the timing.

Once you've organized the workshop content and activities into a workable sequence, the next task is to come up with realistic estimates of how long each part of the workshop is likely to take. If you're new to the game, you might not know, so it can help to seek the advice of an experienced trainer. Add up all the estimates, being sure to include the time needed for breaks, lunch, and transitions between activities and workshop segments.

If the total of your estimates is within the time you have available, that's great. But if you are designing an eight-hour workshop and the total of your estimates comes to nine or ten hours, stop right there because you'll have to find a way to use the time more efficiently, leave something out, or make changes to the design. Even if the time estimates add up to exactly eight hours, you've tried to include too much. Trainers need some "lag" time in an agenda—people do not always arrive on time or come back on time from breaks, and some discussions or activities might go longer than expected. But when you make changes to fit the content and activities more closely to the available time, be sure not to take shortcuts that reduce participant involvement—that's like tossing the baby out with the bath water.

Here are some suggestions for what to do if it appears that you are trying to do too much in too little time:

- *Find out whether more time can be made available.* Just as people sometimes assume that a workshop is the best way to deliver training without stopping to think about whether that's really true, they often assume that a workshop must be a certain length because that's what someone mentioned when the project began: "Let's put together a half-day workshop on this," "I'd like a day of training on. . . ." The timing might be limited by the learners' availability, budget, and other factors—and then again, it might not. It never hurts to ask whether a half-day workshop could be extended to a full day, or a full day to two days.

- *Consider eliminating one or more of the learning objectives.* That can be easier said than done, especially if the design has already been approved by the stakeholders. But just as a playwright may need to cut out scenes if the play runs too long, you may need to trim the training program by cutting out learning objectives. Think about whether the program is attempting to do too much and take a close look at the design to see whether any of the objectives can be eliminated without affecting the program as a whole.
- *Consider splitting off some of the objectives into a separate training program.* If it's important that people achieve all the learning objectives but the time for the workshop cannot be extended, decide whether some objectives might be addressed separately. For example, a program on running productive meetings might be split in two, with the first workshop addressing the objectives related to planning and preparing for the meeting, and the second addressing objectives related to facilitating the meeting.
- *Consider other delivery methods for some of the content.* In many cases, it's the amount of time that learners need to be together in a training room

Reality Check

One of an instructional designer's biggest challenges is convincing stakeholders of the limits to what can be addressed in a training program. People who are not training professionals usually think of training as delivering content instead of as a learning process. Just as tourists assume they can pack a week's worth of sightseeing into a couple of days, stakeholders sometimes assume that you can pack several days' worth of content into a one-day workshop. Neither the tourists nor the stakeholders are likely to be satisfied with the results.

Address this issue as soon as you realize that stakeholders' original expectations might be unachievable. Make sure that the stakeholders understand what objectives the program can reasonably achieve in the given amount of time and gain their agreement before continuing. Help them see that packing in too much content will only set the program up for failure, wasting valuable resources and leaving everyone unhappy.

or a virtual training room that's important. Extending a one-day training workshop to two days might not be practical if learners can't spare that much sequential time away from their jobs or if they will have to travel to the training site. Examine the program for any content that might be delivered more efficiently in another way, such as an e-learning tutorial, a podcast, on-the-job training, or self-study. For example, for the program on meetings, people might use a self-directed program to learn how to plan and prepare for a meeting so that scarce workshop time can be focused on facilitation and group management skills.

- *Replace some of the activities.* If you have included an extensive case study or complex experiential exercise, look for alternatives that would accomplish the same goals in less time. Just be sure that the replacement activity is still an effective way to help people learn.
- *Use pre-work and between-session assignments.* Look for things that learners could do before the program or between sessions so that workshop time is used more efficiently. For example, ask learners to complete self-assessment questionnaires before training begins and read case studies between sessions instead of during the workshop.

If You Don't Have Enough Time

- Find out whether more time can be made available.
- Think about eliminating or splitting off learning objectives.
- Replace some of the activities with less time-intensive alternatives.
- Use other delivery methods, pre-work, and/or between-session assignments for some of the content.

5. Identifying Visuals, Media, and Training Aids

The Chinese proverb says that a picture is worth a thousand words. But let's make that: A well-chosen picture or visual is worth a thousand words.

Bob Pike,
Creative Training Techniques

Check What You Know

The director of a nonprofit community organization that provides English-language courses, child care, and other services to newly arrived immigrants is planning a workshop for new volunteers. Which of the following would be the most effective way to provide essential information that the volunteers need about the organization's goals and programs?

1. ____When the volunteers arrive, there is a television monitor showing a film clip with images of students learning in an English-language class, children in the day care program, and other activities. After introductions, the director gives a brief presentation to explain the organization's goals and provide an overview of its programs, using slides to reinforce and support what she is staying. Then she answers questions and leads a brief discussion of the ways in which volunteers would like to become involved.
2. ____When the volunteers arrive, they find folders on the tables with detailed handouts describing each of the organization's programs, the budgets, and related statistics, along with full-color photographs of people involved in various activities. The director opens the workshop by introducing herself and suggesting that the volunteers use the material to follow along on the handouts while she makes her presentation. When she is finished, she asks whether they have any questions.
3. ____The director comes prepared with a detailed PowerPoint presentation that includes bullet points to accompany her description of each of the organization's programs and detailed statistics and budget figures. At the beginning of the presentation, she hands out folders with copies of the slides and uses a laser pointer to help the volunteers follow along on the slides as she reads the information aloud. At the end of the presentation, she elicits questions from the group.

The first example illustrates the use of visual aids in a way that would be likely to stimulate the volunteers' interest and help them learn about the center's programs. In the second example, the packet of handouts, which would be helpful to reinforce the presentation after it was over, would probably distract people's attention while the director was speaking. In the third, the slides do not support the presentation—they *are* the presentation. They are likely to be too crammed full of information to see easily, and while the hard copies of the slides might be useful if they were handed out at the end of the presentation, they are unnecessary and might be distracting while the volunteers are listening to the director.

You already know that people do not learn well by simply listening to someone talk. In fact, research indicates that most people understand and remember far more when what they hear is reinforced and supported by what they see. Visuals help trainers capture and hold people's attention; convey information more quickly; increase understanding; and reinforce, emphasize, and illustrate points.

Visuals, media, and training aids comprise a broad category that includes anything that supports the training: PowerPoint slides, flip charts, whiteboards, video and audio, props, and handouts. When used properly, they can make a workshop far more interesting and greatly increase people's ability to learn; when overused or used inappropriately, they can be annoying, distracting, and even interfere with the learning process.

One of the important tasks in structuring a training program is to decide where to use visuals, media, and training aids and which ones to use. Below is an overview of what you might need. In Chapter 8, you'll learn more about developing and obtaining these important training aids and materials.

- *Slides*. Even a little familiarity with the use of PowerPoint and techniques of creating slides allows a training designer to develop graphically interesting slides that can be used to illustrate concepts, relationships, and processes; present photographs, drawings, statistics, the steps in procedures, and diagrams; provide instructions for an activity; summarize, emphasize, and reinforce key learning points; and more.
- *Flip charts*. A big pad of paper on an easel and a set of colorful marking pens are a trainer's most useful tools. Flip-chart pages can be used to capture ideas and key points from discussions; provide instructions for activities; illustrate concepts or procedural steps; and more. They can

be posted on the wall, providing ongoing reminders or quick references during the session. Learners can use them to record points from brainstorming activities and group discussions.

- *Whiteboards.* Whiteboards, on which trainers write with erasable marking pens, can be used instead of flip-chart pages to illustrate points and capture ideas from discussions. Their disadvantage has always been that whatever is written on them disappears with a stroke of the eraser. But some of the newer whiteboards allow trainers to make handout-sized printouts of what was written on them. Because you may not know what kind of whiteboard—if any—a trainer will have available, it's best to let the trainer decide whether to use a whiteboard in place of a flip-chart page.
- *Video.* Short films video add interest to a training program, are good ways to demonstrate the right—and wrong—ways to do something, and can be excellent ways to kick off discussions. Today's technology has made it easier and less expensive to produce simple videos (as evidenced by the phenomenal success of YouTube). Many excellent, professionally produced videos are commercially available for purchase or rental. You might be able to find free video clips or short films, and you can sometimes use excerpts from movies or news programs (being careful to honor copyrights). You can also use video as a tool to give participants immediate feedback on their behavior. In a presentation skills workshop, for example, videos of learners' practice presentations help them see what they do well and what they need to improve.
- *Audio.* Trainers can use audio to illustrate points, provide content, or trigger discussions. For example, in a course on telephone communication skills, the trainer might play a dialogue between a customer and a service agent, then ask learners to critique it. Podcasts that people can listen to while they're on the bus or on the treadmill at the gym can substitute for pre-workshop reading—learners can hear the details of a case, gather background information on the topic, or hear questions the trainer wants them to think about before the workshop.
- *Props.* Many training activities involve the use of props—anything from a buzzer that learners hit when they have the right answer in a game or

a ball that they toss around as they brainstorm ideas to the materials and equipment needed for a demonstration. Used properly, props can liven up training, increase understanding, illustrate points, or help learners practice new skills. Like other training aids, too many props, props that are difficult to use, or props that are used at inappropriate times can be distracting and annoying.

- *Handouts.* Handouts include any written materials the trainer gives to participants before, during, or at the end of training. Handouts might include the program objectives and agenda, key learning points, discussion guides, readings, worksheets, follow-up activities, job aids, a reading list—anything that supports and reinforces training. You might design a full set of handouts and provide them to the trainers in electronic form so they can be easily printed out, or you might merely explain what handouts the trainer needs to provide. Depending on the number and uses of handouts, they might be given to participants one at a time during training or in a packet or workbook at the beginning of the program.

  But handouts can (excuse the pun) easily get out of hand. I've attended workshops during which the trainer has handed out a binder of materials so huge that it was almost impossible to use or to lug around. Use common sense when deciding what handouts participants need. Consider encouraging trainers to distribute any material that participants will not actually use during the workshop in electronic form, after the workshop is over.

- *Posters and pictures.* A trainer once told me that she thinks of posters and pictures as "wall candy." Attractive, interesting visuals that can be produced ahead of time and posted on the wall can liven up the room and help to illustrate important processes, procedures, and concepts. Posters and pictures give people something to look at before the workshop starts and during breaks, and they serve as reminders of key learning points during the session.

6. Preparing a Preliminary Agenda

Check What You Know

What's the purpose of a workshop agenda? What information should the agenda include?

____

____

____

____

Once you've determined the sequence of topics and activities, the next step is to develop a preliminary agenda—an overview of the topics and activities and the sequence in which they'll be covered. The preliminary agenda is like the checklist used to make sure that a building is sound before adding the sheetrock, paint, flooring, and finishing touches. It serves as a guide—a sort of working outline—for developing materials.

The preliminary agenda helps you do the following:

- Make sure that everything flows smoothly.
- Make sure that every topic and activity has a clear purpose linked to the objectives.
- Double-check the timing and make adjustments so that breaks do not fall in awkward places.
- Make sure that you've identified the visuals, media, and training aids that the trainer will use at each point in the workshop.

Here is one way to prepare an agenda:

1. If you haven't already done so, list the topics and activities in order, grouping them into workshop segments, including the opening and the

closing. For each segment and each activity within a segment, write a brief statement of the purpose.

2. Determine where the trainer will need to make a transition from one topic, activity, or segment to another and note the transitions on the list.
3. Indicate where breaks and lunch will fall. For workshops of more than two and a half hours, people need at least one ten-to-fifteen-minute break in the morning and one or two in the afternoon; for a full-day workshop, they need a lunch break of at least forty-five minutes. Instructional designers often try to save time by squeezing lunch into half an hour, but in reality, people need time to freshen up, eat, check their messages, and freshen up again before returning to the workshop. If you need to find more time in the day, consider a "working" lunch, where participants engage in a discussion while they eat—but even with a working lunch, include at least twenty minutes for personal activities.
4. Add start/stop times for each segment, for each activity, for each break, and for lunch. This is one of the most crucial tasks in developing the preliminary agenda because it helps you make sure that your original estimates are realistic.
5. Indicate points at which visuals, media, or training aids will be used.

To Prepare an Agenda

1. List the topics and activities in order, grouping them into workshop segments.
2. Determine where the trainer will need to make a transition from one topic, activity, or segment to another and note the transitions on the list.
3. Indicate where breaks and lunch will fall.
4. Add start/stop times for each segment, for each activity and break, and for lunch.
5. Indicate where visuals, media, or training aids will be used.

As you check the timing for the workshop, remain alert for "red flags" that signal possible problems. Is any segment likely to use too much time? Does an activity fall at an awkward time? Have you left some lag time in case the trainer wants to let a productive discussion go on a little longer, there is an equipment malfunction, or something else happens that eats into workshop time? I usually build in three to five minutes of lag time at the end of each segment and after each complicated activity. I also assume an extra five minutes of down time at the beginning of the workshop and a few extra minutes when people come back from breaks and lunch. If things move more quickly than expected, the trainer can add an optional activity—and learners seldom mind finishing early.

If you are short on time or do not have enough content and activities to fill the time, make the necessary changes now, before developing the materials.

Here is an excerpt from the first part of an agenda for a workshop on meetings. This agenda assumes a workshop day that runs from 8:30 to 4:30, with two fifteen-minute breaks and a working lunch. Times are approximate.

Sample Workshop Ageda

Segment	Time	Workshop Segment	Visuals
1.	20–30 min.	MODULE INTRODUCTION	
	Welcome and introductions (activity)	Slide: Welcome	
	Discussion: Why meetings matter		
	Objectives, agenda, ground rules	Slide: Objectives	
		Flip-chart page: Agenda	
	Logistics		
2.	45–60 min.	WHAT MAKES MEETINGS WORK	
	Types of meetings		
	Discussion: When meetings are not needed	Video	
	Activity 1: Meetings That Work (10–15 min.)	Slide: Meetings That Work	
	Activity 2: Reflection (10–15 min.)		
3.	45–60 min.	PLANNING PRODUCTIVE MEETINGS	
	Discussion: Reasons for planning		
	Planning steps		
BREAK (15 min.)			
(3, cont.)	Activity 3: Planning a Meeting (15–20 min.)	Slide: Planning Steps	
	Activity 4: Reflection (10–15 min.)		

Build in Flexibility

When you design a training program, you have the needs and characteristics and needs of a "typical" audience in mind. But you can never count on the audience being "typical." Each group of learners has its own unique qualities. One group might have more experience and know more about the subject than another; one might be more "talky" than another; the learners in one might prefer to do things slowly and methodically, while those in another finish activities quickly and become impatient if the trainer doesn't move on.

Make it easier for trainers adapt the workshop for different groups by suggesting content or activities that could be skipped or truncated; including some supplementary content; and including a few optional activities. Also help trainers make a workshop more relevant for a specific group by adding stories, examples, and activities of their own.

Boris and Marietta's Progress

It's Friday morning and Boris and Marietta have just finished putting the finishing touches on the preliminary agenda for the e-mail workshop. They are about to send it to the HR director so he can send it to the CEO as promised. Here's what the first part of their agenda looks like.

Segment	Time	Workshop Segment	Visuals and Aids	Notes
1.	9:00	OPENING (30 min.)	Slide: Welcome	
		Introductions (activity)		
		What's wrong with e-mail; consequences (discussion)		
		Objectives		
		Agenda	Flip-Chart Page: Agenda	
		Ground Rules		
		Logistics		
2.	9:30	STANDARDS (25 min.)		
		Activity: Advice to Colleague		
		Standards	Slide: Standards	
		Company Policy (discussion)	Handout: Policy	

Quick Quiz

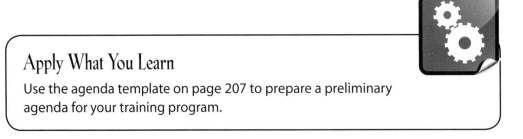

List the three to five key learning points from this chapter that will be most helpful to you.

____

____

____

____

____

What's Next?

During the process of structuring the training program, you will start to determine—if you haven't done so already—what materials the program requires. In the next chapter, you will learn how to identify and develop those materials, and how to keep yourself organized so that everything is there on workshop day.

Apply What You Learn

Use the agenda template on page 207 to prepare a preliminary agenda for your training program.

Answers to Exercises

THINK ABOUT IT

Which strategy or strategies would be effective if you find that you have too much to cover in the time available for a one-day workshop that is scheduled to run from 8:30 to 4:30?

1. ___ Add time by starting the workshop at 7:30 and going until 5:30.
2. _X_ Replace one or more time-consuming activities with activities that requires less time but are still effective ways of helping people achieve the learning objectives.
3. ___ Determine which learning objective requires the most time and eliminate it.
4. _X_ Use another delivery method, such as e-learning, a webinar, or self-study, for some of the content.
5. _X_ Determine whether some of the objectives could be split off into a separate training program.

Check What You Know

The director of a nonprofit community organization that provides English-language courses, child care, and other services to newly arrived immigrants is delivering a workshop for new volunteers. Which of the following would be the most effective way to provide essential information that the volunteers need about the organization's goals and programs?

1. _X_ When the volunteers arrive, there is a television monitor showing a film clip with images of students learning in an English-language class, children in the day care program, and other activities. After introductions, the director gives a brief presentation to explain the organization's goals and provide an overview of its programs, using slides to reinforce and support what she is staying. Then she answers questions and leads a brief discussion of the ways in which volunteers would like to become involved.
2. ____ When the volunteers arrive, they find folders on the tables with detailed handouts describing each of the organization's programs, the budgets, and related statistics, along with full-color photographs of people involved in various activities. The director opens the workshop by introducing herself and suggesting that the volunteers use the material to follow along on the handouts while she makes her presentation. When she is finished, she asks whether they have any questions.
3. ____ The director comes prepared with a detailed PowerPoint presentation that includes bullet points to accompany her description of each of the organization's programs and detailed statistics and budget figures. At the beginning of the presentation, she hands out folders with copies of the slides and uses a laser pointer to help the volunteers follow along on the slides as she reads the information aloud. At the end of the presentation, she elicits questions from the group.

Agenda Template

Title of Workshop: ____________________

Item	Time	Workshop Segment	Visuals and Aids	Notes
1.				
2.				
3.				
4.				
5.				
6.				
7.				
8.				
9.				
10.				

8

Developing Materials and Validating the Program

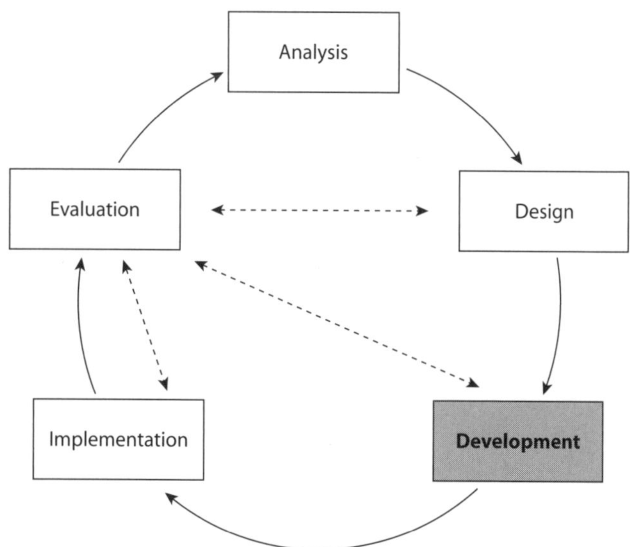

Development Stage of the ADDIE Model

Check What You Know

Boris and Marietta are pleased to learn that the CEO is happy with the workshop agenda. "I also think that it looks very good," the HR director tells them. "When do you think we'll be ready to schedule a pilot?"

But Boris and Marietta were not ready to answer that question—they'd never developed materials for a workshop, so they weren't sure exactly what they needed to do. "Can we get back to you on that in a couple of days?" Marietta asked.

"Let me know by Tuesday if you can," the HR director said. "The CEO is anxious to get going."

How will Boris and Marietta know what materials they need to develop or obtain and how long everything will take? What are some of the things that they need to keep in mind about the workshop materials? What's a pilot, and why do they need to run one?

____

____

____

____

____

____

In the last chapter, you learned that a preliminary agenda for a training program is a little like the framework for a house. Once a contractor has finished the framework, installed the pipes for plumbing and the wires for electricity, put on the roof, and installed the windows and doors, there are still a million things to do before the house is ready for the new occupants. In the same way, once you've finished the framework, there are still a million things to do before a training program is ready for the learners. Those are the tasks involved in bringing the program to life by creating—or obtaining—the materials the program requires, and running a pilot, or a test, to make sure that everything works as planned.

Here's what's in this chapter:

- Using a training materials work plan
- Developing participant materials
- Developing trainer materials
- Developing slides
- Identifying materials for activities
- Validating the training program

1. Using a Training Materials Work Plan

Check What You Know

What does a training materials work plan do for you? What should a work plan include?

____

____

____

____

____

____

We started this book with a discussion of the importance of planning for the success of a training program. Let's revisit that topic. Most workshops require lots of different kinds of materials—participant handouts, trainer notes or script, slides, videos, props, case studies, assessments, materials for activities, visual aids, such as slides and posters; materials for activities, such as case studies or props; media, such as videos; and more. There are lots of tasks to be done to develop, produce, or purchase those items, which is why you need a plan if you hope to stay organized and make sure that everything gets done on time.

Like any project plan, a training materials work plan should specify exactly what materials the program requires, indicate where specific items will come from, and establish deadlines. A good plan helps to clarify responsibilities and establish expectations for a development team so that everyone knows what he or she needs to do. You can use the plan as a checklist while you work. An excerpt from a work plan is shown on the next page.

Here's one way to go about developing a training materials work plan.

1. Using the preliminary agenda as a guide, list every item that needs to be developed or obtained. The list will typically include all or some of the following:
    - Trainer materials, such as a completed agenda and trainer notes or a comprehensive trainer guide
    - Participant materials, such as handouts and/or a participant workbook
    - A PowerPoint presentation
    - Media, such as videos, video clips, podcasts, or software
    - Assessment instruments
    - Job aids
    - Reference materials, such as procedures manuals or books
    - Game materials and props
2. Identify a source for each item: Does it need to be designed? Written? Produced? Purchased?
3. Decide who will be responsible for developing or obtaining each item.
4. Determine when each item needs to be ready to go.

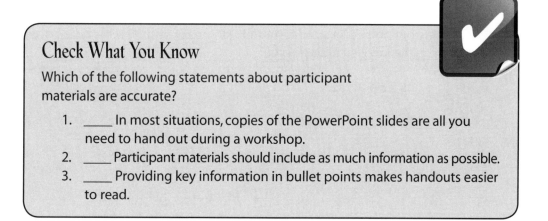

Excerpt from a Training Materials Work Plan

Title of training program: *Team Meetings That Get Results*

Material(s)	Source	Responsibility	Deadline	Notes
Workbook	*to develop*	*Annie F.*	*3-15-09*	
Video	*Vender*	*Martin Y.*	*4-1-09*	*20 min. max.*
Slides	*to develop*	*Annie F.*	*3-15-09*	

2. Developing Participant Materials

Check What You Know

Which of the following statements about participant materials are accurate?

1. ____ In most situations, copies of the PowerPoint slides are all you need to hand out during a workshop.
2. ____ Participant materials should include as much information as possible.
3. ____ Providing key information in bullet points makes handouts easier to read.

Have you ever noticed the way a training room looks at the beginning of the day, when everything is lined up neatly on the tables, and the end of the day, when the place is a mess? Workshops generate an amazing amount of paper—summaries of key learning points, charts and diagrams, guidelines, notes pages, copies of PowerPoint slides, assessment reports, scenarios and cases, job aids—everything that learners need to read, reference, or write on. Much of that material is useful, but overloading participants with unnecessary handouts only ensures a good supply of recycling paper.

Every handout or workbook page should support the learning process by providing information participants need before, during, or after the workshop. If you can't come up with a good reason for including something, leave it out.

Here are some guidelines for developing participant materials that enhance and support learning without using too many trees and too much printer ink:

- Unless the workshop requires fewer than five or six handouts, organize the materials into a folder, binder, or spiral-bound workbook. A well-designed workbook is a convenient way to keep all the material together and makes it easier for participants to use the information after the workshop. Number the pages and make sure that the content and sequence of information is consistent with the presentation.
- Depending on the requirements of the specific program, a participant workbook might include:
    - A table of contents that makes it easy for participants to find specific pages
    - The program purpose and objectives, along with space for learners to write their own objectives
    - Key learning points (or guided note-taking pages on which participants can write the key learning points)
    - Discussion and reflection questions, with space for responses and notes
    - Instructions for activities
    - Note-taking pages
    - Worksheets and templates
    - Job aids
    - Supplementary information for reference after the workshop
    - A reading list
- Make sure that materials are easy to read. Keep the writing to a minimum. Use bullet points instead of long-winded paragraphs. Leave white space on pages. Try not to break pages in the middle of a question or a bulleted item, and start a new page when the topic shifts or a new activity begins.
- Design materials so they have a clean, neat, professional look. You don't have to spend a lot of money

Honor Copyrights and Credit Sources

If you include any material that is under copyright on visuals or participant handouts, be sure to get permission from the copyright holder. Also, when you use research findings, statistics, or other information that comes from others, always credit the source.

Handing Out Copies of PowerPoint Slides

In lieu of or in addition to handouts, some trainers hand out the Notes view of the PowerPoint slides they use to support their presentations. Copies of slides can be helpful, but they do not usually substitute for other handouts. Here are some ways to use them effectively:

- Be selective—hand out copies of only those slides that contain information participants will use in some way during the workshop or for reference after training.
- Instead of handing out full-page versions of slides, print out "Notes" pages or put reduced images of the slides onto pages that have other information and/or room to take notes.
- If participants will use copies of slides only for reference after the workshop, put them at the end of the participant workbook, hand them out at the end of the workshop, or send them out electronically.

on fancy graphics, but fuzzy photocopies, sloppy formatting, and errors are distracting and convey the message that the workshop isn't very important. Use a typeface that's easy to read, and be consistent.

- Don't try to include everything. People learn by writing things down. Limit the amount of information that you include. Instead, provide guided note-taking pages with prompts and questions.
- Put "nice-to-have" in a workbook appendix—better yet, deliver it electronically after the workshop is over.

Think Creatively

Graphics and creative formatting make participant materials attractive and interesting. Columns, boxes, balloons, icons, clip art, even photographs, can make the pages more lively and call attention to tips, strategies, relevant quotes, or things to think about. You'll find design and formatting ideas in "how-to" books and in participant workbooks for other courses. Make copies of pages that illustrate formatting you particularly like and keep them in a file that you can refer to while you work.

3. Developing Trainer Materials

THINK ABOUT IT

If you were delivering a workshop on a subject that was unfamiliar to you, what trainer materials would you need?

____

____

____

____

One of your jobs as an instructional designer is to develop the materials the trainer will use to plan, prepare for, conduct, and follow up the workshop. Trainer materials range from an at-a-glance agenda with a few notes to a detailed trainer's guide that includes instructions for preparing for training, a word-for-word script, and supplementary materials such as answers to frequently asked questions.

It stands to reason that experienced trainers who helped put a program together will need less comprehensive materials than those with little experience who are unfamiliar with it. But if there will be multiple offerings of the same workshop or the program is to be delivered on an ongoing basis, those trainers might deliver only the first few workshops; the trainers who deliver subsequent workshops might be less experienced and know little or nothing about the program. And in many situations, training programs are delivered by people who have extensive knowledge of the subject matter but little or no experience as trainers.

Even if you plan to deliver the program yourself, you may want more than the agenda and a few notes. When I deliver a workshop for the first time,

I use the agenda as a template for a simple script that includes the opening; instructions for the activities; the transitions; the key content and key learning points for each segment; additional details I might need, such as the responses that I expect when I ask questions of the group; and the closing. I don't write everything out—I use bullet points. The level of detail depends on how much I know about the topic and the complexity of the activities.

To determine what materials the trainers are likely to need and identify the level of detail, look at the workshop from the trainers' points of view. Consider the questions below.

Who Will Be Delivering This Training?

Just as you analyzed the learners' needs and characteristics before designing the training program itself, think about the needs and characteristics of the trainers when considering what materials to provide them with. Think about the following:

- Were the people who will be delivering this program involved in any part of the design process?
- What kinds of experience and expertise are the trainers likely to have? Have they delivered similar programs before?
- How complicated is this program? How difficult will it be to deliver?
- How much are the trainers likely to know about the subject matter? How much do they need to know?
- Will this program be delivered by people who are subject-matter experts but not trainers?

For some workshops, even trainers who are unfamiliar with the subject matter and were not involved in the design process might need only a content outline that includes bullet points of what they need to say. But in many cases, trainers need a detailed script that gives them the words to say and tells them exactly what to do at each point in the workshop. For example, trainers might need a script in these kinds of circumstances:

- It is important that the trainer deliver the information in a specific way.
- Different trainers will be delivering the workshop to many different groups, and they need to deliver it consistently from group to group.

- The program will be delivered by subject-matter experts or relatively inexperienced trainers who need a high level of guidance.
- The trainers will know little about the subject matter so they need a high level of detail about what to say.
- The workshop activities are very complex, so trainers need a great deal of guidance to be able to lead them successfully.

What Information Do Trainers Need to Prepare for Training?

Experienced trainers who know how to plan and prepare for training might only need details about specific tasks that relate directly to this workshop, such as what pre-work to assign, special equipment and room requirements, and so on. But training programs that are delivered by subject-matter experts, managers, or trainers with little or no training experience may require a higher level of guidance, including suggestions, guidelines, information, and checklists that help the trainers do the following:

- *Schedule training, choose the right training room, and set the room up properly.* Inexperienced trainers might benefit from scheduling pointers, such as which times of year and days of the week to avoid, tips for what to look for in a training room, and guidelines for setting up the room in a way that encourages interaction and active participation.
- *Prepare participants for training.* Suggestions for notifying participants about the training and assigning pre-work can help less-experienced trainers prepare participants so they are ready to learn when they walk in the door.
- *Adapt the program for a specific group.* Every group has its own unique characteristics and needs. One group might know more about the subject than another; one might be made up of strangers, while in another the participants work closely together. In one workshop, the participants might work through activities much more quickly than in another; in one, people might engage more actively in discussions than in another. Think about whether trainers need guidance for handling different kinds of situations and make changes to tailor the workshop more closely to people's needs.
- *Reserve equipment and prepare materials and supplies.* There are a lot of things to do and keep track of when planning a workshop. A checklist can help trainers make sure that the necessary equipment, materials, and supplies are there on workshop day.

- *Learn about the subject, the participants, and the reasons the training is being held.* Trainers who are unfamiliar with the subject and were not involved in the program design may need suggestions for brushing up on the subject and finding out more about the people who will be attending training. They also need to have a good understanding of the context in which the workshop is being held.

What Supplementary Information Might Trainers Need?

Depending on the situation, trainer materials might need to include the following:

- Answers to questions that participants are likely to ask
- Stories and examples that the trainers can use to illustrate points
- The responses trainers should expect when they ask questions of the group
- How to use cases and assessments that are part of the program
- When and how to use optional activities
- How to establish an environment that is conducive to learning by helping participants feel comfortable and stimulating their interest in the subject
- How to manage the learning group to keep the workshop on track and running smoothly
- How to use visual aids, props, and media
- How to deal with challenges and unforeseen situations

Questions to Ask When Making Decisions About Trainer Materials

- How experienced are the people who will deliver this training? How familiar are they with the subject? The workshop?
- What will trainers need to know about scheduling and setting up the workshop? Preparing the participants? Adapting the program for specific needs?
- What will trainers need to know so that they can prepare themselves to deliver the workshop?
- What supplementary information will trainers need?

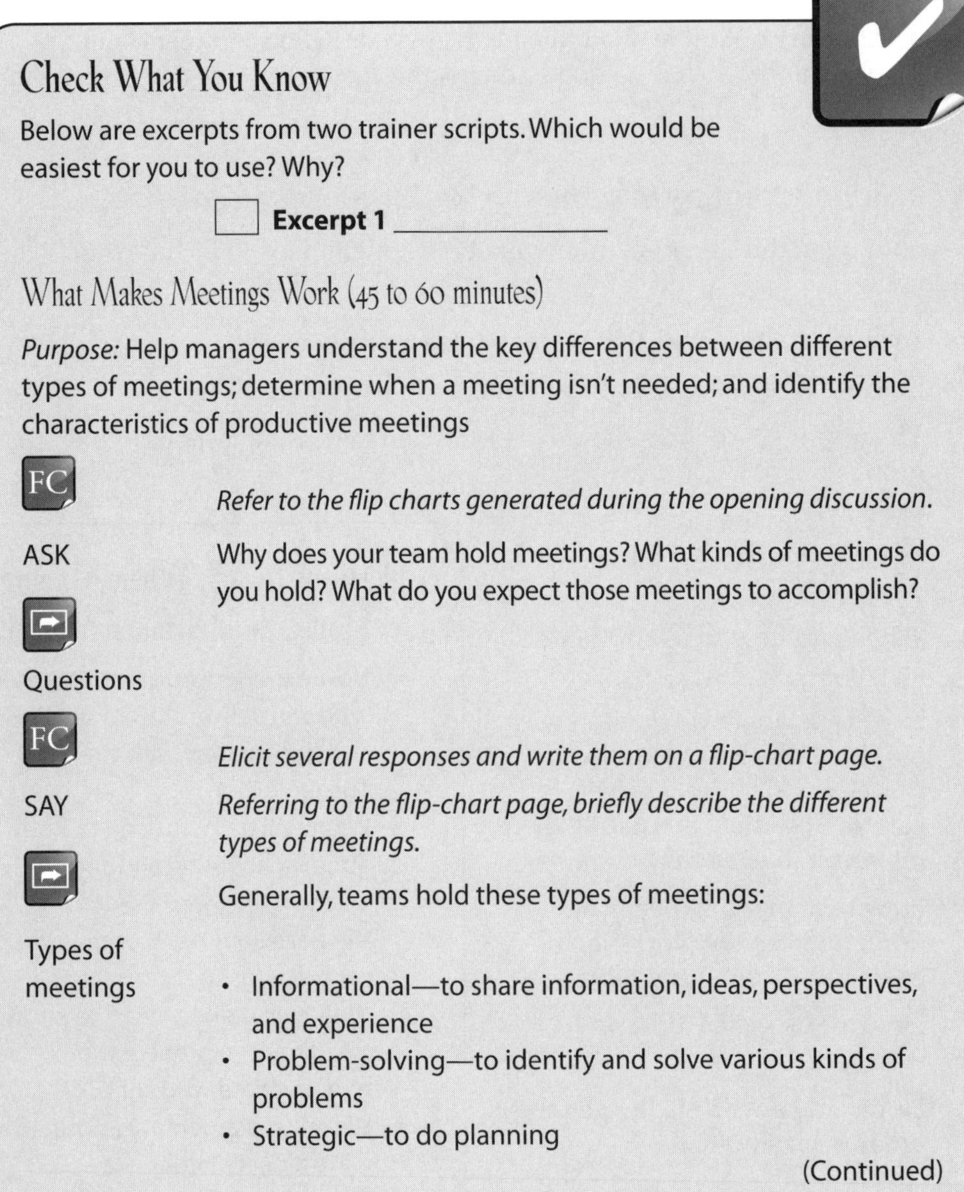

Check What You Know

Below are excerpts from two trainer scripts. Which would be easiest for you to use? Why?

☐ **Excerpt 1** ______________

What Makes Meetings Work (45 to 60 minutes)

Purpose: Help managers understand the key differences between different types of meetings; determine when a meeting isn't needed; and identify the characteristics of productive meetings

FC	*Refer to the flip charts generated during the opening discussion.*
ASK	Why does your team hold meetings? What kinds of meetings do you hold? What do you expect those meetings to accomplish?
Questions	
FC	*Elicit several responses and write them on a flip-chart page.*
SAY	*Referring to the flip-chart page, briefly describe the different types of meetings.*
	Generally, teams hold these types of meetings:
Types of meetings	• Informational—to share information, ideas, perspectives, and experience • Problem-solving—to identify and solve various kinds of problems • Strategic—to do planning

(Continued)

- Decision-making—to discuss issues and make decisions
- Team-building—to discuss process, build community, and increase motivation

SAY Of course, most meetings have more than one purpose. In one meeting, you might need to bring people up-to-date on the status of a project, come up with a solution to a problem, and gain buy-in for a decision. But knowing what you want a meeting to accomplish helps you determine how to structure it—or even whether a meeting is really necessary.

☐ **Excerpt 2** ________________

What Makes Meetings Work

Ask the participants these questions: "Why does your team hold meetings? What kinds of meetings do you hold? What do you expect those meetings to accomplish?" (*Refer to the flip charts generated during the opening discussion. Write their responses on another flip-chart page.*)
Explain that teams generally hold several different types of meetings: Informational—to share information, ideas, perspectives, and experience; Problem solving—to identify and solve various kinds of problems; Strategic—to do planning; Decision making—to discuss issues and make decisions; team building—to discuss process, build community, and increase motivation. (Show the slide)
Most meetings have more than one purpose. In one meeting, you might need to bring people up-to-date on the status of a project, come up with a solution to a problem, and gain buy-in for a decision. But knowing what you want a meeting to accomplish helps you determine how to structure it—or even whether a meeting is really necessary.

Most trainers would find Excerpt 1 much easier to use because it makes it easy to see what they need to say and do. But no matter how elegant a trainer's guide looks, it is useful only if trainers can easily find the information they need when they need it. To make sure that trainer materials are as useful as possible, think of them as "how-to" guides and keep the following in mind:

- Include a table of contents and headings so trainers can quickly find specific information.
- Use icons for quick reference.
- Leave plenty of room for the trainer to make notes.
- Include a detailed "at-a-glance" agenda that shows the sequence of workshop segments, the activities, the estimated time for each segment and each activity, and other key information.
- Instead of using long paragraphs, which are difficult to follow, put information in bullet points with brief introductory statements.
- Use a script format that lets trainers differentiate at a glance between what they are supposed to say and what they are supposed to do and to see what visuals, media, props, handouts, or workbook page to use at a given time.
- Consider including miniature copies of the PowerPoint slides right in the script or on separate pages that the trainer can reference easily.
- Provide electronic versions of the agenda, the script, the slides, and any supplementary material so trainers can easily incorporate any changes that they make to adapt the workshop for different groups.
- Pay attention to the way information is laid out on the page, use a typeface that is clean and easy to read, and make sure that the materials are error-free; trainer materials do not need to be slick and glossy, but they do need to have a professional appearance.

4. Developing the Slides

Check What You Know

Here are three slides that present the same information. Which slide would be most useful? Why?

1. ____To Manage Your E-Mail
   - Get off distribution lists for information you don't need.
   - Ask people to combine their messages.
   - Use the phone for discussions.
   - Direct newsletters to a separate folder.
   - Set up separate mailboxes for certain mail.
   - Manage—and communicate— expectations.
   - A computer to depict " e-mail"

2. ____To Manage Your E-Mail
   - Get off distribution lists for information you don't need.
   - Ask people to combine their messages.
   - Use the phone for discussions.
   - Direct newsletters to a separate folder.
   - Set up separate mailboxes for certain mail.
   - Manage—and communicate—expectations

3. ____Strategies for making it easier to manage your e-mail.
   - Ask that your name be removed from distribution lists if you don't need to receive those messages.
   - Make a request that people who send you e-mail combine the messages that they send.
   - Instead of sending e-mail messages, use the telephone for discussions.
   - Set up a separate folder for the newsletters you receive so that they do not land in your inbox.
   - Set up separate mailboxes for certain mail, such as the mail you receive from clients, along with the mail you receive from team members and from other people.
   - Make sure that you manage—and communicate—the expectations you have about the e-mail messages you send and receive.

How Many Words on a Slide?

In their book, *Point, Click & Wow!*, authors Claudyne Wilder and Jennifer Rotonodo say that high-impact slides meet the following criteria:

- One thought, concept, or idea per slide
- Phrases, not sentences
- No more than six lines of text
- No more than six words per line
- Use a consistent "look." Create a template with consistent graphics, colors, heading fonts, and bullet types so that all the slides appear to be part of the same "family."

PowerPoint slides add interest to a presentation, reinforce key learning points, provide examples to illustrate important points, and help people learn. They can also add flexibility. It's easy for trainers to add, delete, or edit slides, even at the last minute; during a workshop, they can skip or return to slides, depending on the needs of the group.

But slides are intended to support the workshop, not replace the trainer. As mentioned in the last chapter, the ease with which PowerPoint presentations can be created often results in an overwhelming number of slides, many of which are unnecessary. As a result, the trainer ends up clicking through the slides so quickly that participants hardly have a chance to see them. No matter how interesting, clever, or funny, slides that have no clear purpose, that appear unceasingly, one after another, and/or that are too crammed with text or graphics to be legible, are distracting and annoying.

Every slide should support, reinforce, or illustrate something specific, and every slide should be clear and legible. Here are some suggestions:

- *Make sure that slides are consistent with the content that the trainer is presenting*. For example, if the trainer is summarizing the key learning points after an activity, the slide should present the same points, in the same order. Disconnects between what a trainer says and what the slide shows can be confusing.
- *Make slides easy to read*. Participants will not have time to study slides the way they study a handout or a page in a workbook. Make sure that slides can be easily read in the time they are up on the screen. Limit the number of words or images. Use simple fonts, large enough so that words are easy to see, and make sure that images will be clear from the back of the room. Choose a background color such as blue that is easy on the eyes and a contrasting font color that makes the words stand out. Avoid using too many colors on one slide.

5. Identifying Materials for Activities

The package you provide to the people who will deliver training might need to include the materials, such as props, games, and videos, that trainers need for the activities, or you might only be responsible for telling them what they will need. Either way, it's helpful to include a checklist so that trainers can make sure they have everything ready on workshop day. For items that the trainer will supply, include detailed descriptions of what they will need and, possibly, suggestions for where they can obtain specific items.

6. Validating the Training Program

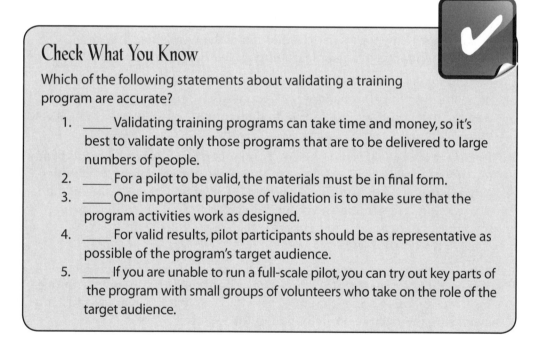

Check What You Know

Which of the following statements about validating a training program are accurate?

1. ____ Validating training programs can take time and money, so it's best to validate only those programs that are to be delivered to large numbers of people.
2. ____ For a pilot to be valid, the materials must be in final form.
3. ____ One important purpose of validation is to make sure that the program activities work as designed.
4. ____ For valid results, pilot participants should be as representative as possible of the program's target audience.
5. ____ If you are unable to run a full-scale pilot, you can try out key parts of the program with small groups of volunteers who take on the role of the target audience.

Before releasing a new product onto the market, a company needs to be sure that it will work as advertised. To do that, the company might run a "beta" test by asking some typical customers to try it out. The results of the test indicate whether the product is ready to go or needs some changes before it is launched.

Testing a training program achieves the same objective—making sure that the program works before handing it over to the people who will run it. That testing process is called "validating" or "piloting" the program. Validating a program can be as simple as running through some of the key activities with a small group of colleagues or as complex as running a full-scale beta test with learners from the target audience.

Validating a program lets you do the following:

- *Confirm the timing of the program as a whole and of each of the activities.* You might need to make changes if the program or any activity runs too long, or if breaks fall at awkward times.
- *Make sure the activities work as designed.* You might need to change or replace an activity that does not achieve the results you expected or that proves to be more or less complex than it needs to be.
- *Check the flow of content and activities.* You might find that some changes in the order of the topics or activities make the workshop flow more smoothly and improve people's ability to learn.
- *Identify anything that needs to be added.* You might discover that people need more information about a topic or a more thorough introduction to an activity. In some cases, you'll find that an important topic or activity has to be added.
- *Identify anything that is unnecessary.* Even when you are very careful during the design process, you might learn that some of the content or activities can be eliminated because they do not add anything of real value to the program. In rare situations, you might even find that an entire learning objective and its related content are unnecessary for the program to achieve the desired outcome.
- *Identify ways to make the program more relevant, interactive, and engaging.* You might discover simple changes you could make that would improve the program by relating it more closely to participants' "real" worlds and increasing their active participation in the learning process.
- *Determine how well the trainer materials, visual aids, media and training aids, and participant materials are working.* You might find that the trainer needs a script instead of notes, or vice versa; that training materials need to be easier to use; that some visuals are not necessary and others are missing; and so on.

The validation process takes time and can be expensive, so it is often skipped. But sending out a new program without testing means that it might be only partially successful in achieving its goals—and, in some cases, that it might not achieve them at all. The more important the program and the more people to be trained, the more important it is to do at least some level of validation.

Here are some guidelines to help you use time and resources wisely when validating a training program:

- If there is not enough time and/or money to run a full-scale pilot of a program, think about what you could do to make sure that everything works as intended. For example, you might be able to try out key parts of the workshop with a few volunteers who agree to take on the role of the target audience. If you are unable to run any sort of pilot, at least try to observe the program the first time it is delivered so you can identify and make changes that would improve it for future groups.
- Use draft materials. There's no use spending a lot of time and money to produce final versions of handouts, workbooks, slides, and other materials for the pilot. Chances are that you will make at least a few changes after testing the program, and you might need to revise some of the materials extensively. Just make sure that the materials are complete enough for a valid test.
- Even for a partial pilot, try for an audience that is as representative as possible of the learners for whom the program was designed. The pilot results might not be valid if the audience knows too much or too little, or has a very different perspective on the subject. For example, you are unlikely to gain much useful information by testing a leadership program designed for executives on line staff, or to test a troubleshooting program designed for experienced help desk staff out on a group of training associates.
- Observe the pilot as if you were a fly on the wall. Unless you have no choice, ask someone else—preferably one of the trainers who will deliver the program—to conduct the pilot so you can sit back and observe what happens. Avoid the temptation to coach or tutor the trainer or the participants. Instead, note places where the trainer has trouble with the material, the participants are unable to come up with key learning points, the flow seems awkward, there are missing or unnecessary visuals, people

seem confused, the timing is off, or activities do not go as planned. When people get stuck or off-track, let them try to work it out for themselves—step in only if it becomes clear that they are not going to find their way on their own.

- Get feedback from the trainer. If someone else conducts the pilot, have a conversation with the person about what worked and what did not. Ask for recommendations for changes to the content, sequence, activities, and/

Boris and Marietta's Progress

Boris and Marietta made a list of everything they thought they might need to develop or obtain for the workshop. They decided to assemble the participant handouts into a binder or a spiral-bound booklet that would include the company's written e-mail policies, summaries of key points, space for learners to take notes, discussion questions for activities, tips, guidelines, and a reading/resource list.

"But what about Jessica and Vittorio, the trainers who will be delivering this workshop?" Marietta said. "I'm not sure what they need."

"Let's ask them," Boris suggested.

"I've done a lot of training," Jessica said. "But I've never done any kind of writing or e-mail workshop before."

"The first few times I do a new workshop," said Vittorio, "it helps to have a pretty detailed script."

Jessica agreed. "Could you also include something about how to prepare people for this workshop—what they should do and think about ahead of time, what they should bring, that kind of thing?"

"And answers to questions that learners are likely to ask?" added Vittorio.

After talking with the trainers, Boris and Marietta revised their original list of materials and made a plan to guide the development process. When the materials were in draft form, they asked Jessica to run a pilot with a small group. They were pleased that it went well. On the basis of what they learned from their observation and the feedback from Jessica and the participants, they made a few changes to the materials, replaced an activity, and deleted some unnecessary content. Their program was ready to launch!

or program materials that the trainer thinks would make the program flow more smoothly and be easier to deliver.

- Obtain feedback from the participants. Make sure that they understand that they are participating in a test of the program, not of themselves. Explain that your goal is to identify what works and what does not, and that you need their frank and honest feedback so that you can make sure the program achieves its goals. Decide how to obtain that feedback. For example, you could interview the pilot participants individually or in groups and/or ask them to complete a questionnaire.

After the pilot, examine the results and determine what actions to take. You might discover that the program is essentially fine, in which case you're ready to prepare final materials and roll it out. More often, you will discover that some, perhaps most, parts of the program might work well, but others need to be changed in significant ways. If the changes are minor, you can make them and then prepare the final materials. But if you make major changes in the sequence of content or activities, or add or eliminate significant components, you might need to run another test.

Sometimes the pilot reveals serious problems with the program that require you to go back to the drawing board. For example, a program that runs much too long or leaves people confused and frustrated might need to be thought through again. You may even need to go all the way back to the analysis stage and start over.

Quick Quiz

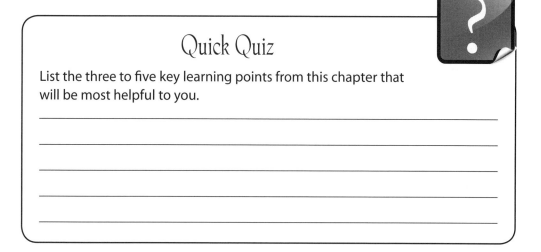

List the three to five key learning points from this chapter that will be most helpful to you.

____

____

____

____

____

What's Next?

The next stage of the ADDIE process is implementation—launching the program. That's where all your hard work pays off in a training program that achieves its goals. The focus of this book, however, is training program design and development, so we will skip that stage and move directly to evaluation, the last stage of the process—but one that is extremely important.

Apply What You Learn

Using the worksheet on page 235, prepare a training materials work plan for your training program.

Answers to Exercises

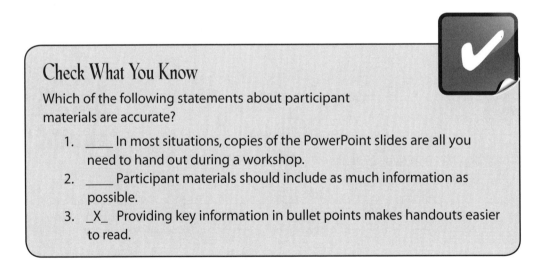

Check What You Know

Which of the following statements about participant materials are accurate?

1. ____ In most situations, copies of the PowerPoint slides are all you need to hand out during a workshop.
2. ____ Participant materials should include as much information as possible.
3. _X_ Providing key information in bullet points makes handouts easier to read.

Check What You Know

Below are excerpts from two trainer scripts. Which would be easiest for you to use? Why?

☐ **Excerpt 1** ______________

This script format would be easier to follow for several reasons: the type size is larger and easier to read; the column format lets trainers see what they are supposed to say or ask and what visual aids they are supposed to use at each point; the short paragraphs and bullets make the text easier to read.

What Makes Meetings Work (45 to 60 minutes)

Purpose: Help managers understand the key differences between different types of meetings; determine when a meeting isn't needed; and identify the characteristics of productive meetings

Refer to the flip charts generated during the opening discussion.

ASK

Why does your team hold meetings? What kinds of meetings do you hold? What do you expect those meetings to accomplish?

Questions

Elicit several responses and write them on a flip-chart page.

SAY

Referring to the flip-chart page, briefly describe the different types of meetings.

Generally, teams hold these types of meetings:

Types of meetings

- Informational—to share information, ideas, perspectives, and experience
- Problem-solving—to identify and solve various kinds of problems

(*Continued*)

- Strategic—to do planning
- Decision-making—to discuss issues and make decisions
- Team-building—to discuss process, build community, and increase motivation

SAY Of course, most meetings have more than one purpose. In one meeting, you might need to bring people up-to-date on the status of a project, come up with a solution to a problem, and gain buy-in for a decision. But knowing what you want a meeting to accomplish helps you determine how to structure it—or even whether a meeting is really necessary.

☐ **Excerpt 2** ______________

In this script, the long paragraphs are difficult to follow and the text is busy and too small. It's also not clear when the trainer should show a slide or use a flip chart.

What Makes Meetings Work

Ask the participants these questions: "Why does your team hold meetings? What kinds of meetings do you hold? What do you expect those meetings to accomplish?" (*Refer to the flip charts generated during the opening discussion. Write their responses on another flip-chart page.*)

Explain that teams generally hold several different types of meetings: Informational—to share information, ideas, perspectives, and experience; Problem solving—to identify and solve various kinds of problems; Strategic—to do planning; Decision making—to discuss issues and make decisions; team building—to discuss process, build community, and increase motivation. (Show the slide)

Most meetings have more than one purpose. In one meeting, you might need to bring people up-to-date on the status of a project, come up with a solution to a problem, and gain buy-in for a decision. But knowing what you want a meeting to accomplish helps you determine how to structure it—or even whether a meeting is really necessary.

Check What You Know

Here are three slides that present the same information.
Which slide would be most useful? Why?

1. ___ To Manage Your E-Mail

- Get off distribution lists for information you don't need.
- Ask people to combine their messages.
- Use the phone for discussions.
- Direct newsletters to a separate folder.
- Set up separate mailboxes for certain mail.
- Manage—and communicate— expectations.
- A computer to depict " e-mail"

The type on this slide is too small and "fancy" to read easily, the items are squeezed together so it's hard to tell where one stops and the other starts, and the graphics, which make the slide too "busy," are distracting.

2. _X_ To Manage Your E-Mail

- Get off distribution lists for information. you don't need.
- Ask people to combine their messages.
- Use the phone for discussions.
- Direct newsletters to a separate folder.
- Set up separate mailboxes for certain mail.
- Manage—and communicate—expectations

This slide is easy to read because the type is large enough, there is some space between items, and the graphics are attractive yet not distracting.

(Continued)

3. ____ Strategies for making it easier to manage your e-mail

- Ask that your name be removed from distribution lists if you don't need to receive those messages.
- Make a request that people who send you e-mail combine the messages that they send
- Instead of sending e-mail messages, use the telephone for discussions.
- Set up a separate folder for the newsletters you receive so that they do not land in your inbox.
- Set up separate mailboxes for certain mail, such as the mail you receive from clients, along with the mail you receive from team members and from other people.
- Make sure that you manage—and communicate—the expectations you have about the e-mail messages you send and receive.

There is so much text that it has been "squeezed" onto the slide, making it difficult to read.

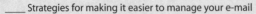

Check What You Know

Which of the following statements about validating a training program are accurate?

1. ___ Validating training programs can take time and money, so it's best to validate only those programs that are to be delivered to large numbers of people.
2. ___ For a pilot to be valid, the materials must be in final form.
3. _X_ One important purpose of validation is to make sure that the program activities work as designed.
4. _X_ For valid results, pilot participants should be as representative as possible of the program's target audience.
5. ___ If you are unable to run a full-scale pilot, you can try out key parts of the program with small groups of volunteers who take on the role of the target audience.

Training Materials Work Plan

Program Title: ____________________

Material(s)	Source	Responsibility	Deadline	Notes

9

Evaluating the Results

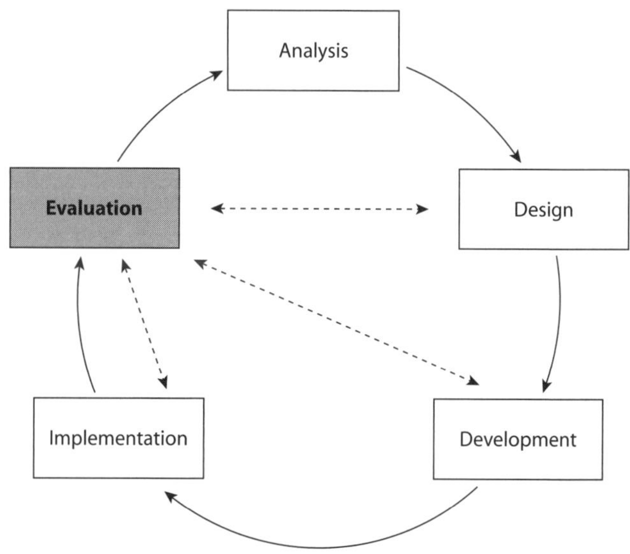

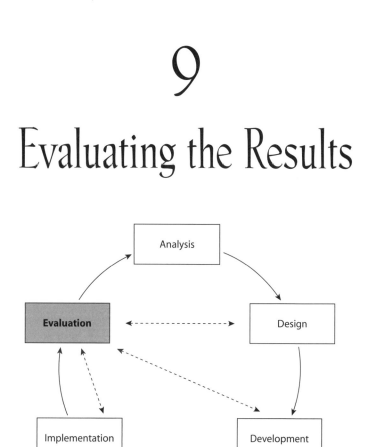

The Evaluation Step of the ADDIE Model

Check What You Know

The HR director told Boris and Marietta that he and the CEO were pleased with the e-mail program and looking forward to its launch with the first group of learners. "There's one more thing," he said.

(*Continued*)

"Once we get the program up and running, the CEO will want to know how well it's working, so we'll need a way to evaluate the results."

"No problem," they replied. "We've already been thinking about the evaluation."

How do you think Boris and Marietta will go about evaluating the e-mail program? What questions should they ask? What criteria should they use?

____

____

____

____

____

____

Looking back on my school years, I remember tests, tests, and more tests. Trying to figure out math problems and guessing at which circles to fill in on the electronic scoring sheets. Frantically trying to finish "blue book" essays before the time was up. Reports. Presentations. All in the service of trying to prove that I had learned something or was able to do something so I could obtain a coveted grade and move on.

I suspect that most of those tests were conducted to find out about *me*—how carefully I'd listened during class, and how well I'd studied—not about how well the course itself helped me to learn. I know that things are changing in education and that there is now more focus on evaluating the teacher's performance, as well as the students'. But what's the function of evaluation when it comes to training? Who and what are being evaluated, and why? That's what this chapter is about.

In this chapter, you'll learn:

- The function of the program evaluation
- The questions an evaluation needs to answer
- How to conduct an evaluation

- The various levels of evaluation
- How to determine what levels to use

Evaluation doesn't deserve to be listed last in the ADDIE model because it takes place in every element and surrounds the instructional design process. Evaluation is a constant guard at the gate of failure.

Chuck Hodell, *ISD From the Ground Up: A No-Nonsense Approach to Instructional Design* (2nd ed.)

1. The Function of Evaluation

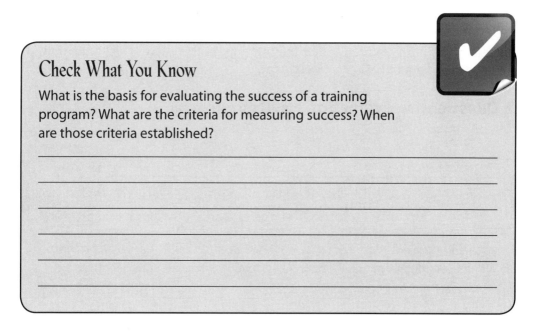

Check What You Know

What is the basis for evaluating the success of a training program? What are the criteria for measuring success? When are those criteria established?

____

____

____

____

____

____

As the quote above explains, don't be misled by the placement of "Evaluation" at the end of the ADDIE acronym. Evaluation starts much earlier in the process and continues after the training has been completed. It's an ongoing question: How will/do we know whether this program has been successful? What changes can we make to improve it?

The basis for evaluation is established when you identify the desired outcome—what the program is intended to achieve—and write the learning objectives that establish the criteria for measuring success. As the program is designed and developed, a continual review of the delivery system, content, structure, learning activities, and materials helps you keep the goal in mind while responding to new information and changes in the situation. Testing the program before it is launched provides a check to see whether it seems to work as designed. Finally, post-training evaluations measure how well the program is working and identify any changes that may need to be made.

Evaluation provides critical information that organizations need to decide whether to continue a program and, if so, whether to change it in any way. The evaluation process takes time, attention, and expertise; for those reasons, it is often neglected, done haphazardly, or skipped altogether. But without evaluation, a program can take on a life of its own, continuing to run month after month, or year after year, without anyone ever stopping to ask whether it actually helps people learn, whether they are using what they learned, or whether there is any evidence that the training has resulted in a change that was worth the organization's investment.

2. Questions an Evaluation Needs to Answer

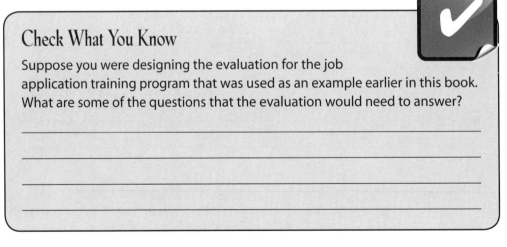

Check What You Know

Suppose you were designing the evaluation for the job application training program that was used as an example earlier in this book. What are some of the questions that the evaluation would need to answer?

____

____

____

____

When a doctor evaluates the success of a treatment, she needs to ask lots of questions: To what degree has a change in the patient's condition taken place? To what degree have the symptoms been alleviated? Is the change likely to be temporary or permanent? Was the change due to the treatment or to something else? If the condition still exists, why? What side-effects, if any, have there been? Are any changes needed in the treatment regime? Should treatment be continued?

Evaluating the success of training also requires asking a lot of questions, such as:

- How did the participants feel about the training? Did they find the program interesting, enjoyable, and useful?
- What did participants learn?
- How well did participants achieve the learning objectives?
- To what degree has change taken place in the learners' performance, behavior, and/or attitudes?
- What unforeseen effects, if any, has training had?
- To what degree has the expected outcome been achieved?
- How well has the outcome of the program met the organization's business goals?
- Does the program provide a reasonable return on the organization's investment?
- If the participants have not achieved the learning objectives, and/or the expected outcome has not been achieved, what are the reasons?
- Should this program be repeated? If so, what changes, if any, are needed to improve it?

Just as the doctor collects information to evaluate the success of treatment by observing the patient, asking questions, and running tests, evaluating the success of a training program requires gathering information by asking questions, observing behavior and the results of behavior, and perhaps, by administering tests.

3. How to Conduct an Evaluation

There are many different methodologies for evaluating training success, and many books have been written on the evaluation process. Perhaps the most commonly used methodology is some version of Professor Donald Kirkpatrick's Four Levels of Evaluation, described in his book, *Evaluating Training Programs*, which is now in its third edition. This method is based on four key questions:

- How satisfied were the participants? Did they find the program interesting? Useful? Enjoyable?
- How much did participants learn? To what extent did they gain knowledge, learn new skills, and/or change their attitudes as a result of the training?
- What change in behavior occurred as a result of the program? To what degree are participants applying what they learned?
- What were the results of training? To what degree was the desired outcome achieved?

The Levels of Evaluation

The first four levels (Kirkpatrick):

- Level 1: What participants thought about the training program
- Level 2: What participants learned from the training program
- Level 3: The extent to which participants are applying what they learned
- Level 4: The degree to which the program achieved the desired results

The fifth level (Phillips):

- Level 5: The organization's return on its investment in the program

Dr. Jack Phillips, a well-respected author and expert on accountability, measurement, and evaluation, has added a fifth item to evaluate that asks, in essence:

- Were the benefits of this training worth the cost?
- What was the organization's return on its investment?

Check What You Know

Which of the statements below are true?

1. ____ Positive participant responses to training are the best indication of how well it has succeeded.
2. ____ People like to be asked for their feedback, but their responses are usually too subjective to be of much use.
3. ____ Participant responses are useful for identifying changes to improve training for future groups.
4. ____ The most common way of evaluating training is to ask participants how well they liked the trainer.

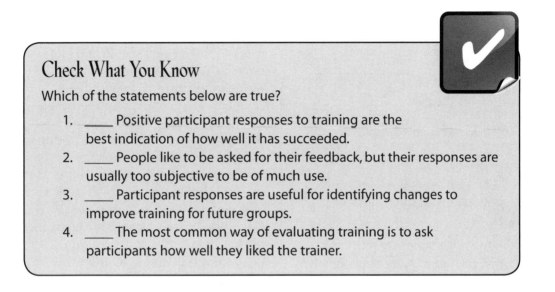

Level 1: Participants' Reaction to Training

A department store where I shop often hands out little questionnaires entitled "How Was the Service Today?" along with the credit card receipt. A few days after I purchased a new computer printer, I received an e-mail that promised to enter my name in a drawing if I would fill out a survey. It seems as if all the people I do business with want to know how I feel about my experience with their service and products. Those questionnaires and surveys are what training professionals commonly call "smile sheets." On the Kirkpatrick model, they are Level 1 evaluations, which answer the question, "How satisfied were participants with their training experience?"

Level 1 evaluations are typically conducted by asking participants to fill out a questionnaire or engage in an informal discussion ("What worked? What didn't?") at the end of the training session or to complete an online survey right after training is over. They are more rarely conducted by interviewing participants in person or on the phone. The questions focus on how well participants thought the program met their needs, how they thought the trainer did, how well the time was used, how well the activities helped them learn, and what changes might improve the program for future groups.

Level 1 evaluations provide helpful information, but it's important to remember that they are very subjective. Participants are usually responding more to the trainer's style and personality than to the substance of the program, and they may be reluctant to make negative comments because they do not want to hurt the trainer's feelings. It's like asking visitors how they like the way you decorated your office—those who think it looks great will say so enthusiastically, while those who think you have questionable taste are likely to smile, say something noncommittal, and keep their real opinions to themselves. And it's important to remember that, although satisfaction with the learning experience can affect the motivation to learn, people can have a great time at a workshop without learning much of anything.

It's not surprising that Level 1 evaluations are by far the most common methods of assessing the success of training—they are the easiest and least costly to administer. Measuring participants' responses to the training experience is only part of the process, however. To truly evaluate a program's success, you need to know what participants actually learned, the degree to which they are applying what they learned, and the business results of the training program.

Level 1 Questions

Whether you use a questionnaire or survey, group discussion, or individual interviews to gather information for a Level 1 evaluation, you will probably be trying to answer these kinds of questions:

- How well did participants think that the program met their needs?
- If training was delivered in a workshop, how did the trainer do?
- How well did the activities help them learn?
- Did any time seem to be wasted?
- Did any information or activities appear to be unnecessary?
- Did anything seem to be missing?
- What changes might improve the program?

The sample "smile sheet" evaluation at the end of the chapter is typical of those that are routinely administered right after a workshop has been completed. Similar questions can be asked electronically, using online survey programs such as SurveyMonkey.

Check What You Know

Which statements accurately describe the purpose of a Level 2 evaluation?

1. ____ To find out what participants learned in the workshop.
2. ____ To find out what people have told others about the training.
3. ____ To find out how well people are able to apply what they learned on the job.
4. ____ To find out the extent to which participants achieved the learning objectives.

Level 2: Participants' Learning

Level 2 evaluations seek to answer the questions, "What have participants learned? To what extent have they achieved the learning objectives?"

You learned earlier that well-written learning objectives contain within them the criteria for measuring success. Here's an analogy: Suppose you order a suit from a tailor in another city. You provide the tailor with certain criteria: style, measurements, fabric, and quality of workmanship. The finished suit can then be evaluated to see how well it meets those criteria.

Similarly, if a learning objective specifies that a loan officer be able to list with 95 percent accuracy the questions that need to be asked of a loan applicant, the loan officer's learning can be evaluated by asking her to list those questions.

There are many methods for evaluating how well someone has learned, including written and performance tests; questionnaires, assessments, and surveys; observation of performance and/or the results of performance; and interviews. The method or methods you use depend on what you are measuring. A written test might be the best way to evaluate how well someone has learned facts; a performance test might be an effective way of determining whether someone can follow a procedure; and a survey might demonstrate whether someone has changed his or her attitudes.

Level 2 evaluations are more time-consuming and costly to develop and administer than Level 1 evaluations. To determine what change has taken place as a result of training, you need a baseline: what people knew or could do, or what their attitudes were, before training. Establishing that baseline usually requires administering some kind of a pretest or conducting some kind of pre-training assessment, which is not always easy to do.

Performance tests, which require observing people perform in a real or simulated situation, are necessarily subjective and may require a great deal of time. And all tests, assessments, and interview questions must be carefully designed to produce valid results.

But perhaps the most important thing to remember about Level 2 evaluations is that they measure what people have *learned*—not necessarily the extent to which they can or will *apply* what they learn. Being able to describe the steps involved in solving a problem doesn't mean that someone can actually use those steps to solve a problem. Being able to give performance feedback in a simulated situation doesn't necessarily mean that the learner will be able to give that same kind of performance feedback to an employee when he is back on the job.

Check What You Know

Check the statements that accurately describe Level 3 evaluations.

1. The primary purpose of a Level 3 evaluation is to measure the extent to which participants:

   ____ remember what they learned

   ____ are applying what they learned
2. A common reason that Level 3 evaluations are seldom done is that:

   ____ they require time-intensive activities

   ____ participants are seldom willing to cooperate
3. Results of a Level 3 evaluation that indicate no significant change in the learners' performance:

   ____ leads to the conclusion that training was unsuccessful in helping people learn

   ____ could mean that people have had no opportunity to use what they learned

Level 3: Participants' Behavior

One of the most important questions to answer about training is, "To what extent are people applying what they learned?" Remember, the primary purpose of training is to change or improve performance in the workplace. So it stands to reason that the most valid evaluation method is an assessment of how well participants apply what they learned.

This level of evaluation is rarely carried out because it requires time-intensive activities such as directly observing on-the-job performance or the results of performance; interviewing managers, colleagues, customers, and others; and/or detailed surveys. Unlike the other evaluation levels, which can be done right after training has been completed, Level 3 evaluations can be done only after the participants have had the time—and opportunity—to apply what they learned.

To complicate matters, if it appears that people have not changed or improved their performance, it can be very difficult to identify the reasons. They may not have had an opportunity to apply what they learned. They might not want to change their behavior. Their managers might not support changes. They might lack the necessary equipment. Changes in organizational structure or procedures might mean they no longer need to use what they learned. For example, the suit the tailor made you might fit just fine and look great on you, but you never wear it because you've left your corporate job to become an artist.

> **Questions for Level 3 Evaluations**
>
> - To what extent are participants applying what they learned? What changes have there been in their performance?
> - Where has their behavior shown the most improvement? The least improvement?
> - To what extent have participants had opportunities to use what they learned? What, if any, obstacles have kept them from using the learning?
> - What, if any, changes have there been in the situation that might be impacting the participants' ability to apply the learning?

If a training project is to have long-lasting value, then it should be connected to specific business results that you can measure. . . . Training projects can't solve every business problem, but a good training project should be able to articulate its goals in ways that can be measured.

"The ADDIE Instructional Design Model,"
www.intulogy.com

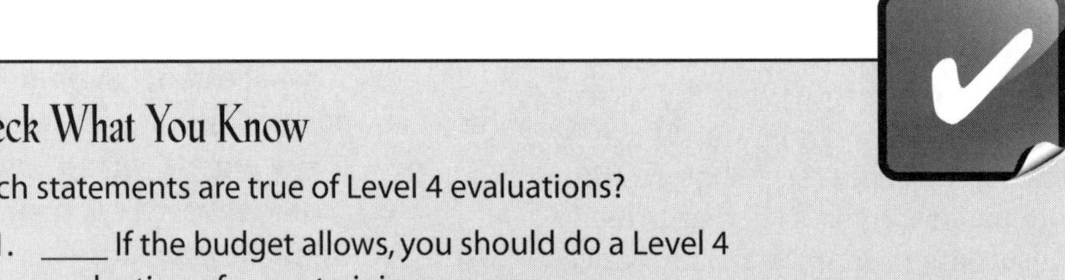

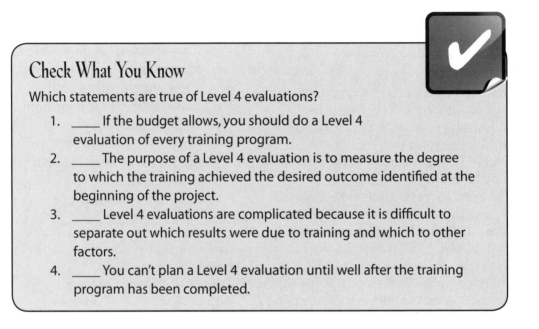

Check What You Know

Which statements are true of Level 4 evaluations?

1. ____ If the budget allows, you should do a Level 4 evaluation of every training program.
2. ____ The purpose of a Level 4 evaluation is to measure the degree to which the training achieved the desired outcome identified at the beginning of the project.
3. ____ Level 4 evaluations are complicated because it is difficult to separate out which results were due to training and which to other factors.
4. ____ You can't plan a Level 4 evaluation until well after the training program has been completed.

Level 4: Results of Training

The design of a training program begins with an examination of the reason that training is needed—sales are slow, there are too many accidents or product defects, customers are complaining, valuable employees are leaving, people are not using meeting time productively. Level 4 evaluations measure how well the training achieved the desired outcome that was identified at the beginning of the project. To what degree has the training improved the company's ability to retain valuable employees or customers? To what extent has employee productivity increased? Has the safety record improved? Are the desired sales targets being met? Are employees more satisfied with their jobs?

There are good reasons why Level 4 evaluations are seldom done or done more or less haphazardly. It's difficult to collect information—even to determine what information should be gathered; there is seldom a clear baseline against which to compare the results; and it's usually very hard to separate out which results, or lack of results, were due to training and which to other factors.

Still, today's organizations are more and more focused on results. They want to be sure that they are using scarce resources where they will do the most good, and training programs increasingly need to provide evidence of their value. As instructional designers, we can't wait to start thinking about how we can measure results until after the program is over. It's too late by then to gather the baseline information we'll need. We must think about all the stages of evaluation right from the beginning of our training project by asking, and asking again: "How will we know whether this program has been a success?"

Level 5: Return on Investment (ROI)

Today's organizations increasingly examine the impact of every activity on business results. But when it comes to training, it can be very difficult to evaluate the actual return the organization receives from its investment. Evaluating the ROI requires calculating all the costs of designing, delivering, and following up the training program—including the salaries and benefits of everyone involved at any stage; consultant fees; facility rental or usage costs; equipment, materials, and supplies; and the cost of participants' time away from their jobs—and then quantifying the program benefits, such as how much time or money is saved by increasing productivity, reducing errors or accidents, retaining customers, and reducing turnover. In fact, according to Bob Pike, evaluating the ROI is not suitable for all learning programs, and only 5 to 10 percent of all programs are evaluated at this level.

Check What You Know

Which of the following statements about deciding which level of evaluation to use are accurate?

1. ____ An important factor to consider when deciding whether to evaluate a program beyond Level 1 is whether there is enough information to provide a baseline against which to measure the results.
2. ____ One way to determine which levels of evaluation to use is to figure out whether the information provided by the evaluation is likely to be worth the cost of collecting and analyzing it.
3. ____ It's usually worthwhile to conduct at least the first three levels of evaluation for every program, even if the program is to be conducted for only one group.
4. ____ Few trainers have the expertise needed to conduct all five levels of evaluation.

How to Determine Which Level(s) to Use

As mentioned earlier, the evaluation process can be lengthy and costly, and it often requires special expertise. At the same time, the information provided by a thorough evaluation can save the organization money in the long run. It's a matter of deciding which level or levels of evaluation are necessary and cost-effective in a given situation. To make that decision, the organization needs to consider these kinds of questions:

- *Whether the program is likely to be repeated*. Obviously, if the program is "special occasion" training that will be delivered only once to only one group of participants, extensive evaluation is unlikely to be worth the time and trouble. A Level 1 evaluation can probably provide enough useful information to help improve the design and delivery of future programs on other topics. But for programs that are to be ongoing or repeated with large numbers of people, more extensive evaluations may be important to ensure that the training is achieving its goals, not wasting everybody's time.

Questions for Determining Which Level to Use

- Is the program likely to be repeated? How often? For how many people?
- Is there a baseline against which to measure what people have learned?
- Is the information provided by the evaluation likely to be worth the cost?
- Is there sufficient expertise to conduct evaluations beyond Level 1?

Boris and Marietta's Progress

Boris and Marietta were ready to design the evaluation of their e-mail program because they had started thinking about it way back at the beginning of the design process. They reviewed the criteria for success—the learning objectives the program was designed to help participants achieve—and discussed ways in which they could gather the information they would need.

"Let's be clear about what we need to know," Marietta said. "I think there are a few key questions: Have the learners' attitudes toward e-mail changed? Are they using their e-mail time more productively? Writing e-mail that meets the criteria they learned in the workshop?"

"Those are good questions," Boris said. "And we should also find out how they felt about the workshop itself. Did the activities work for them? Did they think it covered the right content? Have the right structure? How about the trainer's presentation?"

"We can use an online survey the day after the workshop to get that information," Marietta said. "But how are we going to know whether their attitudes and skills have changed, whether they are using their e-mail time more productively, and whether their e-mail now meets the criteria?"

Boris thought for a moment. "We'll need some kind of baseline. How about sending out a questionnaire before the workshop, asking them about their use of e-mail, and then sending the same questionnaire four weeks after training. We can compare the results."

"And when we send out the questionnaires, we could ask them to send us a few samples of the e-mail they send to clients. You know—before and after. A comparison of the writing samples would give us a good idea about whether they are applying what they learned."

- *Whether there is a baseline against which to measure the results of training*. To determine the extent to which a situation has changed as a result of training, you need detailed information about what it was before training: what people knew, how they were behaving, what attitudes they had, and so on. Baseline information comes from statistics, surveys, tests and assessments, and other sources. That information can be difficult to gather, but it's necessary for accurately determining how successful the program has been.
- *Whether the information provided by the evaluation is worth the cost*. It costs essentially nothing to conduct a Level 1 evaluation; if the baseline information exists, a Level 2 evaluation may be relatively easy and inexpensive. But the higher levels of evaluation may be worth doing only if the program is to be delivered to large numbers of people, is vital to support the organization's business goals or strategic initiatives, and/or is likely to have significant business impacts.
- *Whether there is sufficient expertise to conduct evaluations beyond Level 1.* Even Level 2 evaluations may require expertise in developing and administering valid assessments, and conducting evaluations at the higher levels may be beyond the capabilities of an organization's trainers. For those levels of evaluation, an organization might need to hire an outside consultant who has the necessary expertise.

Quick Quiz

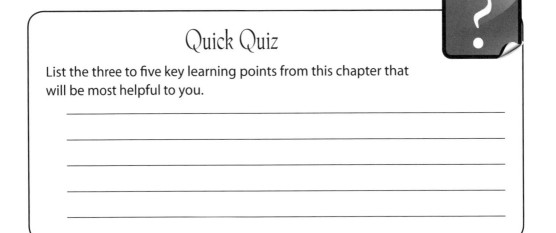

List the three to five key learning points from this chapter that will be most helpful to you.

____

____

____

____

____

What's Next?

You have learned the basic principles that guide the design and development of a training program. In the last chapter of this book, you will learn about the ways in which those principles are applied to the rapidly growing field of distance learning.

Apply What You Learn

Which evaluation method or methods would be best for your training program? Why? What resources would be needed?

- ❑ Level 1, participants' responses to training
- ❑ Level 2, what participants learned from the training program
- ❑ Level 3, the extent to which participants are applying what they learned
- ❑ Level 4, the degree to which the program achieved the desired results
- ❑ ROI, the return the organization received on its investment

Your rationale:

____

____

The resources that would be needed:

____

____

____

____

Answers to Exercises

Check What You Know

Which of the statements below are true?

1. ___ Positive participant responses to training are the best indication of how well it has succeeded.
2. ___ People like to be asked for their feedback, but their responses are usually too subjective to be of much use.
3. _X_ Participant responses are useful for identifying changes to improve training for future groups.
4. _X_ The most common way of evaluating training is to ask participants how well they liked the trainer.

Check What You Know

Which statements accurately describe the purpose of a Level 2 evaluation?

1. _X_ To find out what participants learned in the workshop.
2. ___ To find out what people have told others about the training.
3. ___ To find out how well people are able to apply what they learned on the job.
4. _X_ To find out the extent to which participants achieved the learning objectives.

Check What You Know

Check the statements that accurately describe Level 3 evaluations.

1. The primary purpose of a Level 3 evaluation is to measure the extent to which participants:
   _____ remember what they learned
   _X_ are applying what they learned
2. A common reason that Level 3 evaluations are seldom done is that:
   _X_ they require time-intensive activities
   _____ participants are seldom willing to cooperate
3. Results of a Level 3 evaluation that indicate no significant change in the learners' performance:
   _____ leads to the conclusion that training was unsuccessful in helping people learn
   _X_ could mean that people have had no opportunity to use what they learned

Check What You Know

Which statements are true of Level 4 evaluations?

1. _____If the budget allows, you should do a Level 4 evaluation of every training program.
2. _X_The purpose of a Level 4 evaluation is to measure the degree to which the training achieved the desired outcome identified at the beginning of the project.
3. _X_ Level 4 evaluations are complicated because it is difficult to separate out which results were due to training and which to other factors.
4. _____You can't plan a Level 4 evaluation until well after the training program has been completed.

Check What You Know

Which of the following statements about deciding which level of evaluation to use are accurate?

1. _X_ An important factor to consider when deciding whether to evaluate a program beyond Level 1 is whether there is enough information to provide a baseline against which to measure the results.
2. _X_ One way to determine which levels of evaluation to use is to figure out whether the information provided by the evaluation is likely to be worth the cost of collecting and analyzing it.
3. ___ It's usually worthwhile to conduct at least the first three levels of evaluation for every program, even if the program is to be conducted for only one group.
4. _X_ Few trainers have the expertise needed to conduct all five levels of evaluation.

Sample "Smile Sheet" Evaluation

Title of program: ____

Date(s) of program: ____

Trainer(s): ____

Please check your *primary* reason for attending this program:

❑ Increase my knowledge/skills
❑ Required by my company or manager
❑ Other (please specify): _______________________________________

Overall, how would you rate this program? Please circle the appropriate number:

Excellent		Average		Poor
5	4	3	2	1

The pace of this program was (please check one):

❑ too fast
❑ just right
❑ too slow

The program provided (please check one):

❑ too much information
❑ the right amount of information
❑ not enough information

How relevant was the program to your work?

Very relevant				Not relevant
5	4	3	2	1

How useful will what you learned in the program be?

Very useful				Not useful
5	4	3	2	1

How well did this program meet your expectations?

Very well				Not well
5	4	3	2	1

Please rate the trainer on the following:

	Agree				Do Not Agree
The trainer was well prepared.	5	4	3	2	1
The trainer was knowledgeable.	5	4	3	2	1
The trainer was responsive to participants' needs, questions, and concerns.	5	4	3	2	1
The trainer presented the material clearly.	5	4	3	2	1
The trainer kept the workshop on track.	5	4	3	2	1
The trainer gave everyone opportunities to participate.	5	4	3	2	1

Please give us your specific comments below:

What did you like most about the program?

____

____

What did you find most valuable?

____

____

What changes would you suggest to improve the program?

Other:

10

Designing Distance Learning Programs

Check What You Know

The Account Services e-mail workshops are going well. In fact, the CEO is so pleased that she has asked the HR director to make the program available to employees in distant locations who are not able to come to headquarters for a workshop.

The HR director tells Marietta what the CEO has requested. "Can you and Boris adapt the training for these groups so that it achieves the same objectives?" he asks.

"I'm sure we can," Marietta says. "Give us a few days to think about it and we'll tell you what we come up with."

When Boris and Marietta were considering the best way to deliver the e-mail training, they learned about the different options for delivering training. Now they need to look at those options more carefully. If you were advising them, what distance learning options would you suggest they consider?

(*Continued*)

What questions do they need to ask to be able to choose the right option or options?

____

____

____

____

____

____

I first experienced the challenges involved in "remote" training during my company's fifth year in business, when we were asked to bring our business writing program to field representatives who were scattered across the country. At that time, there weren't many options for providing training to people who couldn't be gathered together in one place for a workshop. We thought about sending a trainer to a few central locations, but travel costs and conflicting schedules made that solution impractical. We considered sending the field representatives the materials and letting them participate by telephone in one of the workshops we were holding at the company's main offices, but without being able to see the trainer or the other learners, we worried that they wouldn't be able to participate in most of the activities. The solution we came up with was to develop a self-paced workbook that the field representatives could go through on their own while we provided support by reviewing assignments and answering questions by phone.

If we had been facing the same challenge today, we'd have many more options. Technology has greatly expanded—and is continuing to expand—the ways in which to provide training when people are unable to come together in the same locations for a workshop. That's what you'll learn about in the final chapter of this book.

What's in this chapter:

- An overview of distance learning
- Questions for deciding when and how to use distance learning
- Design principles for virtual and remote training programs

Persistent usage of technology-based methods has dramatically shaped the [training] field. As organizations deploy e-learning more frequently, the use of instructor-led learning has diminished. Discrete learning events in traditional classroom settings are gradually shifting to learning experiences that are occurring at the workstation and at the pace of the worker.

From the Executive Summary,
ASTD's *2007 State of the Industry Report*

1. Overview of Distance Learning Programs

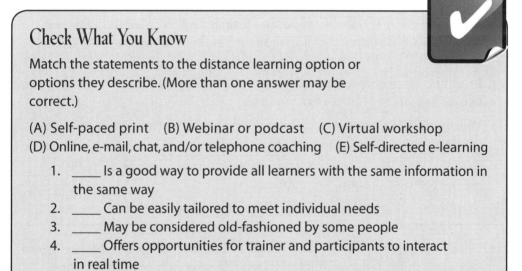

Check What You Know

Match the statements to the distance learning option or options they describe. (More than one answer may be correct.)

(A) Self-paced print (B) Webinar or podcast (C) Virtual workshop
(D) Online, e-mail, chat, and/or telephone coaching (E) Self-directed e-learning

1. ____ Is a good way to provide all learners with the same information in the same way
2. ____ Can be easily tailored to meet individual needs
3. ____ May be considered old-fashioned by some people
4. ____ Offers opportunities for trainer and participants to interact in real time
5. ____ Convenient—allows learners to learn at times and locations of their own choosing

As the workplace changes and new technology becomes more readily available, distance learning, as it is commonly called, is becoming more and more common. According to the ASTD *2007 State of the Industry Report*, the percentage of training programs that are delivered by a trainer in a live, in-person workshop decreased from 74.7 percent in 2004 to 71.36 percent in 2006. Today, the ways in which people work, the global nature of business, and technology are all changing so rapidly that, by the time you read this, distance learning is likely to be even more prevalent, and there are likely to be even more options from which to choose.

Below are descriptions of the most prevalent options for distance learning that are available today. Instructional designers and trainers are increasingly combining these methods to provide a variety of opportunities for people to learn.

- Advanced teleconferencing technology that allow remote learners to participate actively in a live, in-person workshop via audio and/or video links
- Live virtual workshops in which the trainer and the participants meet online, using a conference call, audio technology, and/or chats to communicate with one another in real time
- Print and electronic self-paced programs that learners can take at a time and in a location of their own choosing
- Webinars, or online presentations, some of which offer people an opportunity to ask questions
- Audio and video podcasts that provide information and can include reflective questions and assignments
- Mentoring and coaching via the telephone, e-mail, and/or in online meeting rooms
- Chat rooms, online discussion groups, wikis, and blogs in which learners can share information and learn from subject-matter experts and one another

Some types of distance learning and their features are listed in the following table.

Type of Distance Learning

Type of Program	What to Consider
Self-paced print	Inexpensive to develop and produce; convenient and easy to use; ensures that all learners receive the same information in the same way; not easily updated or customized; may be considered old-fashioned with the rapidly increasing use of technology
Self-paced electronic	Can be expensive and time-consuming to develop (although costs are going down); convenient and easy to use for most people; usually provides all learners with the same information in the same way; can include video and audio; can provide extremely realistic simulations; can be designed with flexibility in mind; appeals to learners who increasingly rely on technology in their day-to-day work
Virtual workshops	Next best thing to bringing trainer and learners together in the same place when learning requires real-time interaction; can include demonstrations and examples; can be relatively inexpensive to design and conduct; requires some technical expertise; subject to the limitations of the technology; can be recorded for viewing by people who are unable to attend "in person"; subject to technical problems that can interfere with the learning process
Webinars	Online presentations that offer most of the same features as virtual workshops but with little or no interactivity; can provide an unlimited number of people with the same information in the same way; can be (and often are) recorded to be viewed at a later time.
E-mail, chat, and/or phone coaching	Allows a coach or trainer to work one-on-one with remote learners; inexpensive and easy to use; easily tailored to an individual's needs
Virtual coaching	Allows a coach or trainer to use web meeting software and the telephone to work with individuals or small groups in an informal, real-time format
Chat rooms	Can be used to support and reinforce other training efforts by allowing learners to share ideas and information with one another in real time
Wiki, blogs, and online discussion groups	Lets learners, subject-matters experts, training professionals, and others share best practices, ideas, and other information
Podcasts	Helpful for providing factual information and examples; easy and inexpensive to produce; easy to use; no interaction or feedback; can be used to support and expand other forms of training
Videos	Helpful for providing factual information and examples; can be expensive to produce and difficult to change; easy to use; provides no interaction or feedback; can be used to support and expand other forms of training

Using Virtual World Technology for Training

The most recent advances in the use of technology for training come from technology that allows designers to create virtual worlds in which people can interact with one another and complete tasks in real time using an "avatar"—a computer-generated image that represents themselves. In these virtual worlds, learners can communicate with gestures and body language as well as their voices. Learners use multiple senses—visual, auditory, and kinesthetic—as they tackle problems and practice tasks in simulated situations that are sometimes more realistic than those that can be presented in a classroom.

2. Deciding When and How to Use Distance Learning

Check What You Know

Below are descriptions of situations in which distance learning is needed. Which one of the following might be the most cost-effective distance learning program for each of the situations? Why?

A. A series of live, instructor-led virtual workshops
B. One-on-one coaching using telephone and e-mail
C. e-Learning program supported by real-time chat sessions with a subject-matter expert

1. ____ A manager has requested training in report-writing skills for a bank auditor who works in a distant state.

____

____

2. ____ Twelve members of a leadership team who are based in different locations (some in different countries) have requested training to improve the ways in which they solve problems and make decisions.

____

____

3. ____ All the supervisors and managers in a large health care organization with branches in nearly every state need to learn how to create a harassment-free workplace.

____

____

Like any other training program, all the forms of distance learning have their advantages and disadvantages, some of which you learned about in Chapter 4. Some are more costly than others; some take more time to develop; some are more effective than others in certain situations and for certain subjects; and many require a level of technological expertise that few instructional designers currently have.

Deciding what forms of distance learning are best to meet specific needs in a given situation, consider these kinds of questions:

- *What's the budget?* As you already know, some e-learning programs can be expensive to develop; even a self-paced print program can be costly if you need to hire instructional writers, editors, graphic artists, and typographers. If you think that a more expensive option is the best way to meet learners' needs and achieve the desired outcome, you might need to come up with a proposal to justify your recommendation.
- *How urgent is this program?* If the training must be delivered quickly, you'll have to forget about programs using sophisticated courseware that require months of design and development time. A speedier option might be a virtual workshop, which you may be able to put together relatively quickly by using a web meeting service. But keep in mind that to be successful, virtual workshops may require special design expertise and

Questions for Deciding When and How to Use Distance Learning

- What's the budget?
- How urgent is this program?
- What technical expertise is available?
- How many people are to be trained?
- What's the subject matter?

learning time on the part of trainers who are used to delivering training in a classroom.

- *What technical expertise is available?* You might need a lot of help if you plan to use a delivery system that requires technology. Some types of programs, such as structured online coaching and virtual workshops, can be designed, set up, and conducted relatively easily. But most distance learning programs, such as e-learning that provides learners with interaction and feedback, virtual workshops that use gaming technology, and complex simulations require high levels of technological expertise. If you do not have the necessary expertise in-house nor the funds to hire a consultant, you'll need to select an option with fewer technological requirements.
- *How many people are to be trained?* There is no doubt that asynchronous distance learning programs can be the most practical way to train large numbers of people. There's no limit to the number of learners who can take a self-paced print or e-learning program, for example, listen to a podcast, or watch a webinar. As mentioned earlier, those types of programs have the added benefit of ensuring that everyone receives the same information in the same way, which can be important in some situations. One of the key considerations is whether the cost of development is worth the investment.
- *What's the subject matter?* Distance learning is no substitute for bringing people together in the same room when they need to be able to share ideas, collaborate on activities, explore issues, and practice communication, problem solving, negotiating, and similar techniques. Virtual workshops are close cousins to live, in-person workshops, but as you learned in Chapter 4, they are not the same. People can't communicate with one another as easily and as quickly, for one thing. Asking and answering questions is more difficult. Trainers can't pick up visual cues that indicate the mood of the group and the level of attention and

engagement, nor can they make on-the-spot adjustments in the content and structure to respond to learners' needs. e-Learning programs, even those that provide a lot of feedback, are also not good substitutes for live, in-person training for subjects that require human interaction. The same goes for other forms of distance learning.

3. Design Principles for Virtual and Remote Training Programs

Check What You Know

Which of the following statements about distance learning are accurate?

1. ____ Like any other training program, a distance learning program must be based on relevant, meaningful learning objectives to achieve the desired outcome.
2. ____ The most significant difference between designing a distance learning program and designing a live-in person workshop is that you are unlikely to be able to learn much about the audience.
3. ____ Because people will not be sitting together in a training room, you can present information in larger chunks in a distance learning program than in a live in-person workshop.
4. ____ Remote and virtual training programs should provide enough variety to meet the needs of people with different learning preferences.
5. ____ The same visuals that work well in a live, in-person workshop usually work just as well in a virtual workshop.

The good news is that it's not necessary to learn an entirely new set of design principles for distance learning. Nearly everything that you have learned in this book about designing training programs to achieve a specific outcome applies to the design of distance learning. The key differences are in the way the program is structured, the types of activities you use to help people learn, and the program materials. While those are significant differences, they do not alter the fact that a successful training program is based on a thorough assessment of the need, a clear understanding of the desired outcome, and learning objectives that specify what people will be able to do when training is completed.

When designing distance learning programs, keep the following in mind:

- *Keep the focus on the learners.* Distance learning should be as learner-focused as a live, in-person workshop would be. Instead of simply presenting information that learners passively listen to, read, or view, provide opportunities for learners to interact with the material so that they discover things on their own and relate what they learn to their own experiences. For example, use the kinds of discussion questions you learned about earlier in this book to help learners discover the key learning points, and include activities that help learners apply concepts and techniques to real and simulated projects. Even a podcast can include questions that help people think about what they are learning and suggestions for applying what they learn.
- *Provide variety.* Like any other form of training, remote and virtual training programs should provide enough variety to meet the needs of people with different learning preferences. For example, you might include an audio component with a self-paced workbook or use video clips in an e-learning program. Also, vary the activities so that they do not become monotonous.
- *Make instructions crystal-clear.* People can't get the full benefit from activities if they don't know what they are supposed to do. It can be difficult for people to ask questions in a live virtual workshop or when they are attending a workshop via teleconferencing, and in those situations, the trainer lacks the visual cues that might indicate that learners are confused or have misunderstood something. Clear instructions are even more important in an asynchronous program in which participants might skip important activities or do them incorrectly because they can't ask questions right away.

- *Include check-ins or checkpoints.* One of the primary challenges for trainers who are conducting virtual workshops is how to know whether participants are paying attention, engaged, and comprehending what they are learning. Participants in a virtual workshop are much more likely to remain focused on the program if they know they will be asked to do something. Build in opportunities for the trainer to poll the group from time to time, ask learners to respond to questions, and encourage learners to share ideas so people are less likely to multi-task or step away from their computers to get a cup of coffee.

Designing Virtual and Remote Learning Programs

- Keep the focus on the learners.
- Vary the activities.
- Make instructions crystal-clear.
- Include check-ins or checkpoints to help trainers and administrators keep people engaged and focused on the program.
- Use schedules and assignments.
- Present content in manageable "chunks."
- Adapt the visuals to the medium.
- Use technology to support and extend the value of self-paced training.

- *Recommend making a schedule and giving assignments.* To help people stay focused when they are taking self-paced programs, suggest that the trainer or administrator ask them to commit to a schedule when they begin the program and include assignments that they will be expected to submit at certain points as they work.
- *Present content in manageable "chunks."* As you learned earlier, "chunking" is the process of breaking down content so that people can learn it more easily. That's even more important for distance learning because there are liable to be lots of distractions in the environment. In virtual workshops, it's hard to hold people's attention for extended periods of time, and few people have the time or the concentration to work on self-paced learning for long periods. In all distance learning situations, it's important to break the content down into self-contained modules that participants can complete in one sitting, and then to break the content in each module into chunks of manageable size.
- *Adapt the visuals to the medium.* Visuals can be very useful ways to convey information in any training program, and distance learning is

no exception. But visuals that work perfectly well in a live workshop might not work as well in a virtual workshop, and graphics that are very effective in a printed workbook might show up differently or take too long to load in an e-learning program. Be sure that the visuals you use help to support the learning process, not distract from it.

- *Use technology to support and extend the value of asynchronous programs.* Learning on your own can be a lonely endeavor. When designing self-paced print and e-learning programs, suggest ways in which trainers and learners can create a learning community that offers opportunities for participants to interact with one another, subject-matter experts, and others: chat groups, websites, blogs, wikis, discussion groups, and forums in which people can talk, share ideas, or find more information.

Boris and Marietta's Progress

Boris and Marietta have finished the distance learning version of the e-mail program. Here's what they came up with:

- They found an off-the-shelf e-learning tutorial that covered many of the learning objectives and could easily be adapted to fit Account Services' employees' needs.
- They developed a three-module virtual workshop that the company's trainers would deliver at periodic intervals during the next twelve-month period and which would be recorded so employees could view it at any time.
- They arranged to have the new e-mail policy sent out to everyone in the company, along with a description of the training options available and guidelines that team leaders and managers could use to help employees select the best option. They decided to send out a discussion guide that would help team leaders facilitate a discussion of the policy with their team members.
- They set up a website where people could share information and obtain help with e-mail-related issues.

Quick Quiz

List the three to five key learning points from this chapter that will be most helpful to you.

___

___

___

___

___

Apply What You Learn

Imagine that you have been asked to adapt your training program for distance learning.

1. What would the distance learning program look like? Which forms of distance learning could you use?

   ___

   ___

   ___

   ___

(*Continued*)

2. What resources—time, money, expertise, technology, etc.—would you need to develop this distance learning program?

____

____

____

____

3. What are some of the things that you would need to consider and keep in mind while developing this program?

____

____

____

____

Answers to Exercises

Check What You Know

Match the statements to the distance learning option or options they describe.

(A) Self-paced print (B) Webinar or podcast (C) Virtual workshop (D) Online, e-mail, chat, and/or telephone coaching (E) Self-directed e-learning

1. A, B, possibly E Is a good way to provide all learners with the same information in the same way

2. C, D, (and possibly E) Can be easily tailored to meet individual needs
3. A May be considered old-fashioned by some people
4. C, D Offers opportunities for trainer and participants to interact in real time
5. A, B, E Convenient—allows learners to learn at times and locations of their own choosing

Check What You Know

Below are descriptions of situations in which distance learning is needed. Which one of the following might be the most cost-effective distance learning program for each of the situations? Why?

A. A series of live, instructor-led virtual workshops
B. One-on-one coaching using telephone and e-mail
C. e-Learning program supported by real-time chat sessions with a subject-matter expert

1. __B__ A manager has requested training in report-writing skills for a bank auditor who works in a distant state.

   This is an individual need, so it can be best met with an individual response.

2. __A__ Twelve members of a leadership team who are based in different locations (some in different countries) have requested training to improve the ways in which they solve problems and make decisions.

   The team members will learn best with opportunities to interact and collaborate.

(Continued)

3. __C__ All the supervisors and managers in a large health care organization with branches in nearly every state need to learn how to create a harassment-free workplace.

The size of the audience and the subject matter indicate that e-learning would be appropriate and cost-effective; the chat sessions would extend the value of the e-learning program.

Check What You Know

Which of the following statements about distance learning are accurate?

1. __X__ Like any other training program, a distance learning program must be based on relevant, meaningful learning objectives to achieve the desired outcome.
2. ____ The most significant difference between designing a distance learning program and designing a live-in person workshop is that you are unlikely to be able to learn much about the audience.
3. ____ Because people will not be sitting together in a training room, you can present information in larger chunks in a distance learning program than in a live in-person workshop.
4. __X__ Remote and virtual training programs should provide enough variety to meet the needs of people with different learning preferences.
5. ____ The same visuals that work well in a live, in-person workshop usually work just as well in a virtual workshop.

Resources

The publications, websites, and associations on this list are only a few of the excellent resources available for learning more about training. You can find books that are out of print at Amazon.com and other online booksellers. Also check out www.HRDPress.com, www.AMACOM.com, and www.Pfeiffer.com for other great training resources.

Publications

Allen, Michael. *Michael Allen's 2009 e-Learning Annual.* San Francisco: Pfeiffer, 2009.

ASTD. *2007 State of the Industry Report*. Alexandria, VA: Author. (www.astd.org)

ASTD. *2004 Competency Model*. Alexandria, VA: Author. (www.astd.org)

Barbazette, Jean. *The Art of Great Training Delivery: Strategies, Tools, and Tactics.* San Francisco: Pfeiffer, 2006.

Biech, Elaine (Ed.). *90 World-Class Activities by 90 World-Class Trainers*. San Francisco: Pfeiffer, 2007.

Biech, Elaine. *Training for Dummies*. Hoboken, NJ: John Wiley & Sons, 2005.

Bloom, Benjamin S. *Taxonomy of Educational Objectives*. Boston: Allyn and Bacon, 1984.

Bowman, Sharon L. *Training from the Back of the Room!: 65 Ways to Step Aside and Let Them Learn*. San Francisco: Pfeiffer, 2008.

Caffarella, Rosemary S. *Planning Programs for Adult Learners* (2nd ed.). San Francisco: Jossey-Bass, 2002.

Clark, Ruth Colvin, and Mayer, Richard E. *e-Learning and the Science of Instruction* (2nd ed.). San Francisco: Pfeiffer, 2008.

Clark, Ruth Colvin, and Kwinn, Ann. *The New Virtual Classroom: Evidence-Based Guidelines for Synchronous e-Learning*. San Francisco: Pfeiffer, 2007.

Conley, Chip. *PEAK: How Great Companies Get Their Mojo from Maslow*. San Francisco: Jossey-Bass, 2007.

Covey, Stephen R. *7 Habits of Highly Effective People*. New York: Simon and Schuster, 2004.

Diamond, Robert M. *Designing and Assessing Courses and Curricula*. San Francisco: Jossey-Bass, 1998.

Fee, Kenneth. *Delivering e-Learning: A Complete Strategy for Design, Application, and Assessment*. London: Kogan-Page, 2009.

Foshay, Wellesley; Silver, Kenneth; and Stelnicki, Michael. *Writing Training Materials That Work: How to Train Anyone to Do Anything*. San Francisco: Pfeiffer, 2003.

Gardner, Howard. *Multiple Intelligences: New Horizons in Theory and Practice*. New York: Basic Books, 2006.

Gargiulo, Terrence L. *Once Upon a Time: Using Story-Based Activities to Develop Breakthrough Communication Skills*. San Francisco, Pfeiffer, 2007.

Gargiulo, Terrence L., Pangarkar, Ajay M., and Teresa Kirkwood. *The Trainer's Portable Mentor*. San Francisco: Pfeiffer, 2008.

Goad, Tom W. *The First-Time Trainer.* New York: AMACOM, 1997.

Goman, Carol Kinsey. *The Nonverbal Advantage: Secrets and Science of Body Language at Work*. San Francisco: Berrett-Koehler, 2008.

Gronstedt, Anders. Training in Virtual Worlds: Training Technology and e-Learning. *Infoline, 25*. Alexandria, VA: ASTD, 2008.

Gupta, Kavita. *A Practical Guide to Needs Assessment* (2nd ed.). San Francisco: Pfeiffer, 2007.

Hodell, Chuck. *ISD from the Ground Up: A No-Nonsense Approach to Instructional Design* (2nd ed.). Alexandria, VA: ASTD, 2006.

Kirkpatrick, Donald L., and Kirkpatrick, James D. *Evaluating Training Programs: The Four Levels* (3rd ed.). San Francisco: Berrett-Koehler, 2006.

Knowles, Malcolm S., Holton III, Elwood F., and Swanson, Richard A. *The Adult Learner: The Definitive Classic in Adult Education and Human Resource Development* (6th ed.). Amsterdam: Elsevier, 2005.

Kolb, David A. *Experiential Learning: Experience as the Source of Learning and Development*. Upper Saddle River, NJ: Prentice-Hall, 1984.

Lawson, Karen. *The Trainer's Handbook* (2nd ed.). San Francisco: Pfeiffer, 2006 (updated edition, 2008).

Leatherman, Dick. *Training Trilogy: Conducting Needs Assessment, Designing Programs, Training Skills* (3rd ed.). Amherst, MA: HRD Press, 2007.

Leigh, David. *The Group Trainer's Handbook: Designing and Delivering Training for Groups* (3rd ed.). London: Kogan-Page, 2006.

Mager, Robert F. *Preparing Instructional Objectives* (2nd ed.). Belmont, CA: David Lake Publishers, 1984.

Nadler, Leonard. *The Handbook of Human Resource Developmen*t. Hoboken, NJ: John Wiley & Sons, 1984.

Pike, Robert W. *Creative Training Techniques Handbook: Tips, Tactics, and How-To's for Delivering Effective Training* (3rd ed.). Amherst, MA: HRD Press, 2003.

Silberman, Mel. *Training the Active Way*. San Francisco: Pfeiffer, 2006.

Society for Human Resource Management (SHRM). *2006 Workplace Forecast*. Alexandria, VA: Author. (www.shrm.org)

Stolovitch, Harold D., and Keeps, Erica J. *Telling Ain't Training*. Alexandria, VA: ASTD, 2002.

Thiagarajan, Sivasailam. *Thiagi's Interactive Lectures*. Alexandria, VA: ASTD, 2005.

Thorne, Kaye, and Mackey, David. *Everything You Ever Needed to Know About Training* (4th ed.). London: Kogan Page, 2007.

Weimer, Maryellen. *Learner-Centered Teaching*. San Francisco: Jossey-Bass, 2002.

Wilder, Claudyne. *Point, Click & Wow!: The Techniques and Habits of Successful Presenters* (3rd ed.). San Francisco: Pfeiffer, 2008.

Magazines, Websites, and Newsletters

Websites and the addresses of web publications change frequently. If you are unable to find a magazine, website, or newsletter using the web address on this list, try a web search for an updated address.

Accelerated Learning Network Newsletter: www.accelerated-learning.net

ASTD Learning Circuits articles: www.astd.org/lc

Creative Training Techniques Newsletter: www.creativetrainingtech.com

Don Clark/Big Dog, Little Dog: nwlink.com/˜donclark, bdld.blogspot.com/

eLearn Magazine: www.elearnmag.org

Ignite Newsletter: www.kenblanchard.com/Business_Leadership/Management_Leadership_Newsletter/

www.intulogy.com/library

Learning at Light Speed weblog: www.learningatlightspeed.com

Performance Improvement Journal (PIJ): www.ispi.org (resource center)

Peter Honey and Alan Mumford's Learning Styles Questionnaire, www.peterhoney.com

www.roiinstitute.net

Training and Development: www.astd.org/TD/

Training magazine, Lakewood Publishers: www.trainingmag.com

Associations and Organizations

These associations and organizations are excellent resources for people in the training field, offering information, learning opportunities, publications, blogs, conferences, networking, and more.

American Society for Training and Development (ASTD), www.astd.org/

American Management Association (AMA), www.amanet.org

The e-Learning Guild, www.elearningguild.com

International Association of Facilitators (IAF), www.iaf-world.org

International Society for Performance Improvement (ISPI), www.ispi.org

Society for Human Resource Management (SHRM), www.shrm.org

About the Author

Janis Fisher Chan, a writer, editor, instructional designer, and trainer, has been in the training field for more than twenty-five years. As a co-founder of Write It Well (formerly Advanced Communication Designs), a training company that specializes in helping people communicate clearly and work together productively, she designed and conducted a wide range of training programs on topics that ranged from business writing to negotiating and consulted with clients on training-related issues. She is the author of *E-Mail: A Write It Well Guide—How to Write and Manage E-Mail in the Workplace* and other books in the Write It Well series; Pfeiffer's *An Academic Manager's Guide to Meetings*; and the American Management Association's self-study courses *How to Manage Your Priorities* (2nd ed.); *Delegating for Business Success; Presentation Success*; and *Communication Skills for Managers* (5th ed.). She also served as an instructional writer and developmental editor for the highly acclaimed *Leadership Challenge Workshop, The Five Dysfunctions of a Team* Workshop Kit, and other books and training packages for Pfeiffer and other publishers. After receiving her master's degree in theater from San Francisco State University, she returned to the university to complete a post-graduate program in organization development. She lives in Marin County, California.

Index

B

C

D

E

F

G

H

Q

R

S

T

U

V

W